DOOMED

ALSO BY JOHN FLORIO AND OUISIE SHAPIRO

For Young Readers
War in the Ring: Joe Louis, Max Schmeling,
and the Fight between America and Hitler

For Adults
One Nation Under Baseball: How the 1960s Collided with
the National Pastime
One Punch from the Promised Land: Leon Spinks,
Michael Spinks, and the Myth of the Heavyweight Title

Also by John Florio
Blind Moon Alley
Sugar Pop Moon

Also by Ouisie Shapiro
Bullying and Me: Schoolyard Stories
Autism and Me: Sibling Stories

JOHN FLORIO & OUISIE SHAPIRO

DOOMED

On July 14, 1921, Nicola Sacco and Bartolomeo Vanzetti were convicted of armed robbery and murder. After a series of appeals that made headlines around the world, the two men were executed in 1927.

From John Florio and Emmy-award-winning writer Ouisie Shapiro com a monumental nonfiction

Italian Im that

SACCO, VANZETTI, AND THE END OF THE AMERICAN DREAM

ROARING BROOK PRESS
New York

Published by Roaring Brook Press
Roaring Brook Press is a division of Holtzbrinck Publishing Holdings Limited Partnership
120 Broadway, New York, NY 10271 • fiercereads.com

Our books may be purchased in bulk for promotional, educational, or business use. Please
contact your local bookseller or the Macmillan Corporate and Premium Sales Department
at (800) 221-7945 ext. 5442 or by email at MacmillanSpecialMarkets@macmillan.com.

ISBN 978-1-250-62193-1
Library of Congress Control Number 2022931701

First edition, 2023
Book design by Aurora Parlagreco
Printed in the United States of America

10   9   8   7   6   5   4   3   2

For our grandparents

CONTENTS

A NOTE TO THE READER

We have tried to remain as faithful to the story of Sacco and Vanzetti as possible. Throughout the book, dialogue that appears in
quotation marks was taken exactly as it was spoken. Dialogue
that appears in italics is meant to capture the meaning of what the
speaker intended. In those instances, we have used our own words
to convey the original idea.

DOOMED

April 15, 1920

A workday in South Braintree.

Factory whistles screeching. Hundreds of employees filing into four-story brick buildings.

This was Massachusetts, the center of America's shoe industry. With its assembly lines cranking on overdrive, the state was churning out a pair of women's shoes every second, more than one hundred million pairs of shoes and boots in 1920 alone.

Pearl Street in South Braintree, Massachusetts, circa 1920

On Thursday afternoon, April 15, Frederick Parmenter, the forty-five-year-old assistant paymaster at the Slater & Morrill shoe factory, picked up the corporate payroll from his boss. Like most everybody at the company, Parmenter knew about the recent robberies in the area. He also knew he'd be carrying a lot of cash to the main factory—$15,776.51, enough to pay the company's four hundred employees. The money had been divvied up into two large wooden cases and slid into heavy-gauge steel boxes secured with Yale locks.

Taking no chances, Parmenter made sure to avoid walking alone. He waited for protection, which, in this case, came in the form of forty-four-year-old security guard Alessandro Berardelli. About three o'clock, Parmenter and Berardelli left the payroll office in the Hampton House on Railroad Avenue and, walking briskly, turned left onto Pearl Street.

New Englanders were finally getting a taste of spring. The sun had come out, and temperatures were climbing into the high 40s. Crocuses and daffodils were blooming, and the town's residents had come out of hibernation to take on outdoor projects or relax in the April breeze. A dozen or so construction workers hammered at the ground on the north side of Pearl, digging a foundation for a new restaurant. A man in a dark-colored cap leaned against a fence by the telegraph pole. Electric trolleys and Model T cars made their way through town, and a young guy leaned over the hood of a big, dark, boxy Buick, tinkering with the engine.

At the foot of the Pearl Street water tower, Parmenter and Berardelli ran into mechanic Jimmy Bostock.

There's a problem with the factory motor at Slater & Morrill, Parmenter told Bostock. *I think the pulley is broken.*

Bostock made a note to check the motor, and Parmenter, satisfied that Bostock was on the job, walked past the Rice & Hutchins shoe factory, trailing Berardelli by a few steps.

That's when the gunshots rang out.

Pop! Pop!

The man by the fence, the one wearing the cap, now had a gun in his hand—and chased Parmenter and Berardelli. He grabbed Berardelli's shoulder, spun him around, and fired three bullets into his left side.

Pop! Pop! Pop!

The gunshots echoed throughout the streets. Factory windows flew open. Pigeons fluttered. Onlookers froze, afraid to move.

Berardelli fell to his knees, his bright white shirt turning a deep crimson red.

Parmenter wheeled around, and the gunman shot him in the chest. The paymaster staggered, dropped the cashboxes, and turned to get away, but the gunman shot him again—this time in the back.

There, in the middle of Pearl Street, the two men lay on the ground dying.

The gunman snatched up the payroll boxes and fired another shot into the air.

Pop!

The youngster who'd been tinkering with the Buick hopped into the car and drove over to the gunman. The kid wasn't alone; two guys were in the back seat, each holding a rifle. The gunman jumped inside and continued shooting, this time at employees looking out of factory windows.

Pop! Pop! Pop!

With Berardelli lying on the ground, another bandit sprang out from behind a pile of construction bricks, a pistol in his fist. He leaped onto the Buick's running board and squeezed the trigger, striking Berardelli with a fourth shot. This one tore through Berardelli's right shoulder and punctured his aorta, the chief artery carrying blood from the heart to the rest of the body.

The bandit swung around and took two shots at Jimmy Bostock, missing wide.

The gang of five criminals—the driver, the two guys in the back seat, the gunman by the telegraph pole, and the bandit from behind the bricks—took off, the Buick spraying gravel from the gutter as it sped toward the railroad tracks. To make sure they wouldn't be tailed, one of the crew leaned out of the front passenger window, firing a rifle to his right and left. Another reached out of the back window and dropped a slew of rubber-headed tacks onto the road, no doubt hoping to flatten the tires of any car that gave chase.

Bostock ran over to Berardelli, wiped the blood that was oozing out of his mouth, and begged him to hold on until help arrived.

Please, Alessandro. Hang in there.

But that final bullet was now lodged in Berardelli's abdomen, and the damage couldn't be undone. Berardelli died in Bostock's arms, leaving behind a wife and two children.

The whole episode had taken less than a minute.

Seconds later, the Buick reached the railroad crossing on Pearl— at virtually the same time as an oncoming train. Firing a fusillade of bullets at the gatekeeper, the gunman yelled out the window.

Raise the gate! Up! Up!

With bullets pinging off the gatehouse walls, the gatekeeper, Michael Levangie, did as he was told.

The Buick bolted past the moving train and swept out of town, taking corners on two wheels.

Back on Pearl Street, Parmenter was barely breathing. A few residents wrapped him in a horse blanket and put him in an ambulance, which was soon speeding to Quincy City Hospital, its engine straining under the stress. Doctors removed a bullet from his gut, but it had torn through a large vein and the bleeding could not be stopped.

Parmenter died at five o'clock the next morning. Like Berardelli, he left behind a wife and two children.

The only hard evidence at the scene was a handful of shell casings from a .32-caliber pistol. Those casings were traced to three different manufacturers, but all of them were large companies with very wide distribution.

Remington.

Winchester.

Peters.

The police also found the cap of the first gunman—he'd dropped it in the street—but it was a common style and could have been worn by pretty much anybody.

A group of boys gathered up the tacks from the road, five pounds' worth.

Desperate for leads, the state police released a description of the gang: "All dark complexioned except one. No overcoats, dark suits, and probably foreigners except the light-haired chauffeur."

Two men were dead.

And the cops had virtually nothing to go on.

PART ONE

AMERICA

1908–1920

1

Nicola Sacco: Life Is Beautiful

On April 12, 1908, the White Star Line's S.S. *Romanic* pulled into Boston Harbor. As the ship maneuvered toward the dock, the fifteen hundred passengers jammed the decks with hats and kerchiefs covering their heads. In the crowd, a wide-eyed, olive-skinned sixteen-year-old boy from Italy, Nicola Sacco, stood alongside his older brother Sabino. He was still queasy from the choppy seas and itching to plant his feet on solid ground.

American ground.

This was the United States, where anything was possible. Subways now moved people underground; Americans spoke on telephones, drank Coca-Cola, and shaved with Gillette razors. The wealthy lit their homes with electricity and swept their floors with portable vacuum cleaners. Nicola couldn't believe his good fortune to land here, the place where Henry Ford, Cornelius Vanderbilt, and so many others had built industrial empires. To the young Nicola— smart, hardworking, good with machines—this was the land of dreams.

Nicola and Sabino had come all the way from Torremaggiore,

a medieval town in southern Italy, twenty miles from the Adriatic Sea. Their father, Michele, had pulled Nicola out of school after the third grade and put him to work in the family vineyard. Nicola had loved roaming the outdoors—sometimes he even slept in the vineyard to keep the neighbors' animals from eating the vines. When the sun came up, he'd pick fruits and vegetables and bring them to his mother, Angela; then he'd watch, fascinated, as his father harvested local wheat with a big threshing machine. Now, more than four thousand miles from home, Nicola could still conjure up the pungent smell of the olive trees and hear the singing birds that used to follow him across the fields.

Those were happy days.

Still, when Sabino, now twenty-three, came back from the Italian army with his head full of wild ideas about going to America in search of bigger things, Nicola saw a once-in-a-lifetime opportunity.

Immigrants seeking a better life arrive in America, circa 1908.

And so here he stood, his feet about to kiss American soil.

This new country was already so different from home. In Torremaggiore, two-story mud-and-stone houses, most of them whitewashed to soften the effects of the scorching sun, lined a maze of narrow, winding streets. Here, in the gritty, overcrowded city of Boston, sturdy granite warehouses sprawled along the wharf. And the port bustled with activity, a sure sign that America had progressed beyond Torremaggiore, where farmers were living in the past, still producing wheat and wool with little mechanization beyond a threshing machine.

But the America that was awaiting Nicola and Sabino—and millions of other immigrants—was a far cry from the one they'd imagined. The richest ten percent of Americans owned nearly all of the country's wealth. Unskilled laborers found work where they could, often in coal mines, textile and steel mills, and garment factories, where the wages were pitifully low and the working conditions unsafe. It wasn't uncommon to find children as young as ten slaving for twelve hours a day in canneries and sweatshops.

Scared and hopeful in the same breath, Nicola and Sabino took a train to Milford, a town about thirty miles west of Boston, where a family friend had offered to put them up. Nicola knew little English, but it didn't matter; Milford had a sizable Italian community. There were even streets named after Italian towns—Naples, Genoa, Florence, Ravenna—and one paid homage to Italian explorer Christopher Columbus.

Standing only five-six and weighing a mere 145 pounds, Nicola wasn't built for hard labor, but his energy and enthusiasm made up for his lack of muscle. He quickly found work from fellow Italians; as a water boy on a construction site he made $1.15 a day, and within three months, he was promoted to pick-and-shovel crewman for $1.75 per day. In the winter, when New England was too cold for outdoor work, he kept at it, eagerly tackling manual labor jobs at a local textile mill.

But Sabino, despite being the one who'd hatched the idea of coming to America, was homesick. He'd found employment in a foundry, but the unbearable working conditions—the furnaces burned at over two thousand degrees Fahrenheit—drove him back to Italy. Before long, he was again working in the open air with his father, eventually becoming mayor of Torremaggiore.

Before sailing home, he gave Nicola some advice.

Learn a trade, he told him. *There's a big difference between skilled and unskilled labor. If you have a skill, you'll always do well.*

Nicola didn't have to go far to follow his brother's guidance. Milford, like so many other industrial towns in eastern Massachusetts, was turning out shoes at a record pace. So Nicola saved his money—fifty whole dollars!—and signed up for a three-month program that trained newly arrived immigrants on shoemaking machines. He soon mastered the edge trimmer, a device that spun circular knives at up to eleven thousand revolutions per minute. He practiced, over and over again, cutting leather soles to size by running their edges along the knives. Even with the machine's help, it was an exacting job because the shape of each sole had to match its mate precisely. Missing by even a thousandth of an inch would ruin a pair of shoes. But Nicola had good eyes and steady hands. And the ambition to stick with it.

Comfortable in his Italian community, he found work at the Milford Shoe Company. There he sat every day on his stool by

Workers cut leather in a Massachusetts shoe factory.

the window, trimming sole after sole, obscured by the cloud of dust spewing from the buzzing knives.

One evening in 1911, Nicola, now twenty, went to a dance, a benefit for a paralyzed accordion player. It was a festive affair filled with music, punch, and speeches—but Nicola, always clean-cut, didn't drink, nor did he dance. As he made his way through the crowd, he caught sight of a small, slender young woman standing off to the side. She probably lived in Milford, but he'd never seen her before.

What's your name? he asked.

Rosa, she said. *Rosa Zambelli.*

Nicola kept asking questions, methodically piecing together the woman's journey to America. She'd come from the Lombardy region of northern Italy. Her parents had immigrated to the United States when she

A young Nicola Sacco

was young, leaving her in an Italian convent to be educated, but they sent for her a few years later. Now sixteen, she lived in Milford with her family.

Nicola looked at her again, at her red hair, fair skin, and dark eyes—and at the sweet innocence on her face.

So this is how it felt to fall in love.

Can I see you again, Rosina? he asked, calling her by his new special name for her.

In the many months that followed, they saw each other in the evenings and on weekends. And then on November 28, 1912, with permission from Rosina's father, they married. They rented an apartment next door to the Catholic church in Milford, and the following year, Rosina gave birth to their son, Dante.

For Nicola, life was beautiful.

Until five years later, when America entered the Great War.

■ ■ ■

Bartolomeo Vanzetti: Stranger in a New Land

On June 19, 1908, a horde of passengers raced to the top deck as the ocean liner *La Provence* glided into New York Harbor. There, rising out of the water and pushing its way through the fog, stood America's symbol of freedom, the Statue of Liberty. At the mere sight of the copper-and-steel goddess, the people whooped, cheered, and wept with joy.

One of the ship's passengers was a gangly twenty-year-old named Bartolomeo Vanzetti. Alone, with no family or friends waiting for him, he made his way up from the bottom deck and into the fresh air—and was instantly struck by the sight of the great city.

"New York loomed on the horizon in all its grandness and illusion of happiness," he wrote years later. "I strained my eyes from the steerage deck, trying to see through this mass of masonry that was at once inviting and threatening the huddled men and women in the third class."

The ship docked in the harbor. After having their papers quickly checked, the first- and second-class passengers were let off in lower Manhattan. Bartolomeo and his fellow travelers in steerage boarded a ferry for inspection at Ellis Island. This was their first stop in America.

Like so many other immigrants, Bartolomeo had come for a better life. His mother, Giovanna, had died seven months ago, and what better place was there to start anew?

This was the land of the free, the place of so many dreams.

It was also utter mayhem.

Immigration officers barked orders at the worn-out foreigners. Bartolomeo's shipmates, many still sick from the roiling seas, wore tattered suits and tired expressions as they shuffled along. Children wept, hiding their faces behind their mothers' skirts, bewildered by the strange and scary scene.

Nobody knew where to report, and the officers appeared cold and uncaring.

Get in line, they shouted at Bartolomeo. *Where are your papers? Hand them over, now!*

What were they saying? Didn't they know he barely spoke English? Didn't they realize he had just spent seven days crammed into the dark and musty lower deck, eating leftover meat, friendless aside from his books?

The officers continued to point and shout, herding the newcomers as if they were livestock, pushing them into different areas of the station. They seemed to take special delight in intimidating the lost, the poor, the disadvantaged—so they preyed on those like Bartolomeo. His melancholy face, high cheekbones, and long, straight nose immediately labeled him a foreigner, and his status as a third-class passenger indicated he had few resources.

Bartolomeo felt as though he'd unwittingly become a specimen in a laboratory. Doctors patrolled the second-floor balcony of the two-hundred-foot-long inspection building, looking down on him and the other foreigners, their purpose an open secret. They were

Main Hall at Ellis Island, circa 1908

scanning the crowd, searching for those who showed signs of illness, ready to brand their lapels with a series of chalk marks and send them back home. And so Bartolomeo and his fellow passengers tried their best to appear healthy, drawing strong breaths, and walking as steadily as their weary legs would allow.

Once inside the Great Hall, Bartolomeo underwent a cursory medical exam. The doctors checked his heart and his lungs, and looked for any signs of smallpox, tuberculosis, yellow fever, or other infectious diseases. Despite being tired, hungry, and thirsty, Bartolomeo passed. He then followed a maze of metal railings to another station, where yet another official fired a battery of questions at him. With a translator at his side, Bartolomeo responded one at a time. *My name is Bartolomeo Vanzetti. No, I'm not married. Yes, I can read and write in my own language. No, I have not*

A young Bartolomeo Vanzetti

been in prison. Yes, I'm ready and able to work. No, nobody is waiting for me. No, I am not an anarchist.

Five hours later, having made it through Ellis Island, Bartolomeo—with exactly thirty-two dollars in his pocket—stood on the southern tip of Manhattan, getting his first up-close look at America. Simply walking those city blocks was a journey through prosperity. Cars and trolleys clamored along the streets, and the forty-seven-story Singer Tower, the tallest building in the world, pierced the clouds. Well-groomed men in top hats and tails strolled into fancy restaurants and swanky clubs. But their wealth obviously was not shared by all: For every tycoon, there were dozens of homeless men sprawled on the sidewalks, and ragtag children foraging for food in alleyways. It was, to Bartolomeo, a living portrait of injustice. Years later, he would call New York "the immense hell pit of the poor and the paradise of the rich."

He would also remember how he felt during those first few hours in a strange new world: "I seemed to have awakened in a land where my language meant little more to the native . . . than the pitiful noises of a dumb animal. Where was I to go? What was I to do? Here was the promised land. The elevated rattled by and did not answer. The automobiles and trolley sped by, heedless of me."

This place, this America, was nothing like home.

Villafalletto, a picturesque hamlet in the north of Italy, had been so serene, so familiar. Bartolomeo's parents were farmers; they raised him, his younger sister Luigia, and his youngest siblings, Vincenzina and Ettore, in a comfortable two-story house with a red-tiled roof. Every summer, he and Luigia spent mornings picking apples and pears from fruit trees and afternoons cooling themselves in the river.

Every day had brought a new adventure.

Those were his favorite times—until 1901, when he turned thirteen. That's when his father, Giovan Battista, sent him away. Instead of exploring the outdoors with Luigia, he was suddenly an apprentice in a pastry shop in the nearby town of Cuneo.

Life is easier when you have a trade, his father had said. *You're not happy now, but you'll thank me when you're older.*

Bartolomeo was miserable. He had been happy going to school, and he was a good student; he loved reading books and filling his head with new ideas. In Cuneo, he slogged his way through fifteen-hour workdays, exhausted and homesick.

But every letter home was met with a stern response from his father to keep at it.

Then one day, Bartolomeo became too sick to work. The knife-like pains he had been feeling in his chest turned out to be pleurisy, an inflammation of the lungs. Realizing Bartolomeo was seriously ill, Giovan Battista gave in and brought his son back to Villafalletto. In 1907, after six bleak years, Bartolomeo finally returned to the family farm—and collapsed into the loving arms of his mother.

Rest, my son, said Giovanna, perched by his bedside, nursing him back to health. *Breathe the fresh air. You'll be better soon.*

But he wasn't better soon. It took months for him to regain his health; he couldn't even walk with a cane until weeks had passed. Then, basking in Villafalletto's sunshine and fully recovered under his mother's care, Bartolomeo watched Giovanna fall victim to liver cancer.

And so the roles reversed themselves.

Suddenly, Bartolomeo was the nurse and Giovanna the patient.

For months, he tended to her every need, reading to her, comforting her, trying desperately to keep her alive—but her illness was too invasive and too aggressive to be stopped.

Bartolomeo held his mother as she gasped her last breath. Cradling her limp, shriveled frame was more than he could bear. He spent days wandering in the woods alone, but he couldn't right himself. He wasn't the same. When Giovanna left this world, she took a piece of him with her.

He was desperate to numb his pain, to leave his old life behind.

He had heard promising tales about America—that jobs were plentiful and wages were good.

So he made the decision to put the Atlantic Ocean between him and his grief. The loneliness, however, shadowed him wherever he went. He couldn't outrun the memory of his mother, of throwing that fistful of earth on her coffin, of saying goodbye to the woman who had given him so much love.

Now, standing in downtown Manhattan under the rattling elevated train, Bartolomeo thought about how his father had embraced him at the railway station, weeping and begging him not to go to America. There was no doubt his father was grieving and wanted his oldest son by his side. But it's also possible that he'd wanted to keep Bartolomeo safe from harm. He, too, had come to America as a young man. Maybe he'd also stood on this very pavement, clutching a battered suitcase, wondering how he would survive in a foreign country with no money and few resources.

Bartolomeo had to find work somehow, so he tracked down Giacomo Caldera, a fellow countryman from Villafalletto, who was living on West 25th Street and working as the head cook at a men's club uptown.

I'll get you a job as a dishwasher, Giacomo told him, *and you can live above the club.*

Bartolomeo accepted the offer—how could he not?—but he found no peace, and no sleep, in the cramped, rat-infested attic. To make matters worse, his scarred lungs couldn't tolerate the heat in the sweltering industrial kitchen, nor could his nerves handle the constant commotion coming from the elevated trains, delivery trucks, and street traffic.

Three months later, he left, hoping to find more satisfying work.

The search proved even tougher than he'd thought. He bounced from one restaurant job to the next, laboring fourteen-hour days in steamy, foul-smelling kitchens for as little as six dollars a week— barely enough to feed himself. When he could no longer take the sickening smell of rotting food, he left the city for the open air of the countryside. He wandered through Connecticut and then Massachusetts, taking jobs nobody else wanted. He dug ditches, installed telephone wires, split stones, carried bricks, hammered railroad ties, built dams, just about anything that wasn't in a restaurant kitchen. None of it paid enough to keep him out of poverty.

Bartolomeo quickly learned that in America, Italians were facing discrimination of all kinds. Employers ran want ads with explicit instructions on who should—and shouldn't—apply.

From the *Evening Record* in Hackensack, New Jersey: "WANTED—Pick and shovel men; must have grub-hoe and shovel; $1.75 per day. No Italians need apply. Bogota Fire House."

From the *Washington Times* in D.C.: "UNION BARBER, white; no Italian need apply. 655 Pennsylvania Ave."

And from the *Boston Globe* in Massachusetts: "BARBER—A good chance for business. No Italian need apply."

When his pockets were empty and his savings gone, Bartolomeo went back to New York. After five years in America, he was reduced to begging, sleeping in doorways, and searching for pennies to buy food. Still, he ignored his father's pleas to come home. He wasn't ready to give up on his new country. Thank goodness for his books; as he wandered the city, desperate and homeless, he kept his sanity by reading the words of Leo Tolstoy, Charles Darwin, and Émile Zola.

Bordering on starvation and realizing New York wasn't the

answer, he left again, this time chasing rumors of work back to Massachusetts. In the summer of 1913, he made his way to the small coastal town of Plymouth, where he worked various jobs as a laborer. One job was at the local cordage factory. There, he loaded coils of rope onto freight cars for nine dollars a week. In a few years, a friend moving back to Italy would sell Bartolomeo his fish cart, along with his knives and scales. Happy to become a fish peddler and work outdoors, Bartolomeo would no longer have to labor inside a factory.

The townspeople would come to see him as "a familiar figure on the streets and byways of Plymouth. With his long, walrus mustaches, sparkling and laughing brown eyes, his large soft hat and open shirt, he would become a picturesque character as he jovially pushed his fish cart and cried out: 'Pesce! Pesce!'"—Fish! Fish!

He settled into Plymouth, renting a room from an Italian couple, Vincenzo and Alfonsina Brini. Far from rich, he nonetheless enjoyed living there, especially the Sunday afternoons he spent with the Brini children: Lefevre and Beltrando, who were in grammar school, and Zora, who was just a toddler.

To the young Brinis, Bartolomeo was the Pied Piper—leading them on adventures, instructing them in proper Italian, sharing his love of nature, and encouraging Beltrando in his violin lessons.

Together they would stroll through the woods, picking flowers and berries, or walk alongside the railway tracks, hunting for fallen pieces of coal. How he loved inhaling the fresh air and listening to the children's laughter.

One day, when they were out for a walk, they ran into a group of kids selling fresh mayflowers.

Hey, mister, the youngsters said. *Do you want to buy some flowers? We picked them ourselves.*

Despite having only a few coins in his pocket, Bartolomeo didn't hesitate. *I'll take them all.*

The youngsters, delighted, handed over the bouquet to Bartolomeo, who dropped the last of his money into their grateful, outstretched palms.

When they walked away, Beltrando, not yet ten years old, asked Bartolomeo why he had bought all the flowers when he could have shown his support by taking only one or two.

Those children spent all day picking the flowers, Bartolomeo told him. *They deserve to be rewarded for their effort.*

Poor but happy, Bartolomeo had finally landed on solid ground—he'd found a home and a family in Plymouth.

Until America entered the Great War.

**Beltrando Brini, seventy-nine years old, remembering
Bartolomeo Vanzetti**

March 14, 1987

*He believed in the perfectibility of human nature, some-
thing that does not in fact exist. That was his blind spot. He
treated us with love and respect. And he treated animals the
same way. Once he found a sick kitten in the street, an infec-
tion all over its face; he brought it home, kept it in a box on
the porch, washed its eyes with boric acid and nursed it back
to health.*

*He loved nature, flowers, the sea with the same unadul-
terated love. As we walked in the woods and on the beach
he established in my mind, with his conversation and his
actions, values and virtues that have remained with me ever
since.*

2

The Great War

In April 1917, President Woodrow Wilson declared war on Germany and joined the fight in Europe, which had begun nearly three years earlier upon the assassination of Austrian Archduke Franz Ferdinand. The murder had unleashed aggression across Europe and, eventually, around the world. On one side was Germany, Austria-Hungary, Bulgaria, and the Ottoman Empire; on the other was Great Britain, France, Russia, Italy, Romania, and Japan.

Wilson had resisted joining the conflict. But after German U-boats sank the *Lusitania*, a British ship carrying 128 Americans, and then began targeting U.S. merchant ships, he changed his mind.

Unfortunately for the president, the war in Europe was matched by racial conflict at home.

The country was overwhelmingly white, and throughout the South, segregation was legal. State and local statutes known as Jim Crow laws prevented Black people from attending quality schools, voting, and getting decent jobs. Southern Italians weren't treated much better. Due to their olive-toned skin, they were often written off by many white Americans as poor, illiterate, and capable only of manual labor. In many parts of the United States, southern Italians were confined to the back pews of Catholic churches. In considering ways to restrict immigration in 1912, congressmen openly questioned whether "the south Italian" was "a full-blooded Caucasian."

It was this political climate that allowed Luigi Galleani, a passionate, charismatic revolutionary, to become the most influential anarchist in the United States. Operating out of the factory town of Lynn, Massachusetts, the Italian-born Galleani captivated his Italian comrades by denouncing capitalism, an economic system in which companies and property are owned privately and run for profit. To him, capitalism produced poverty as readily as it did wealth. As an anarchist, Galleani rejected all forms of authority and exploitation. He wanted to end government, which oppressed the people and protected the status quo. Anarchism, he promised, would do away with private ownership and competition. It would free workers to share the riches of the land.

Anarchism had arisen in Italy in the 1870s, and Galleani embraced it while studying law at the University of Turin. The movement crossed the Atlantic with a wave of immigration. It spread quickly, especially among Italians, many of whom were poor and unskilled. By the time Galleani arrived in the United States in 1901, at the age of forty, anarchism had already taken root in America.

Galleani was an imposing figure, with a tall frame and a thick mustache and beard. He was even more impressive when he spoke, mesmerizing his audiences with a booming voice. Galleani's followers, known as Galleanists, considered themselves the voice of the lower classes. They envisioned a society run by the people, one in which mutual respect would replace competition.

Anarchist leader Luigi Galleani

To promote his message, Galleani published the newspaper *Cronaca Sovversiva* (Subversive Chronicle) and put it into as many hands as possible. Both in person and in print, he called for the overthrow of the American government—a capitalist regime—and incited his disciples with a forty-six-page handbook on bomb-making titled *La Salute è in Voi!* (Health is in You). Recognizing that Galleani had the power to trigger a violent revolution, U.S. authorities raided the office of *Cronaca Sovversiva* after war was declared. They tried to shut it down, but Galleani managed to keep distributing the paper to his several thousand readers—and his influence only grew. The government, frustrated and fearful, continued to keep close tabs on him and his followers.

Two of those followers were Nicola and Bartolomeo. Both men supported Galleani's vision, though neither of them felt that violence was the way to achieve it.

Nicola liked what Galleani said about workers standing up to a government that didn't seem to care about them. The more time Nicola spent in the factory, the more convinced he became that America's capitalist system was the worker's enemy, that it kept poor people from making money, and brought even more wealth to company owners. He had learned a trade and landed on his feet, but that wasn't true for millions of other immigrants. American factory conditions were wretched and dangerous. Workers were mangled by machinery and routinely exposed to toxic chemicals, intense heat, and deadly fumes. Regularly inhaling coal dust was giving miners black lung disease. In one textile mill, a spinning machine took hold of the hair of a twelve-year-old girl and ripped off part of her scalp.

Laborers were risking their lives simply by going to work.

Only seven years earlier, in 1911, the Triangle shirtwaist factory had gone up in flames. That disaster could have been prevented, but because of hazardous conditions, 146 people died. Everybody seemed to know the story, how the factory had occupied the top three floors of a building in New York City's Greenwich Village, how the flames shot up through the floors, trapping the people inside, and how the workers—mostly Jewish and Italian women and girls—clutched each other's hands and jumped out of the windows, preferring to fall to their deaths rather than burn.

Nicola looked at those workers' struggles as his own. In his words, "The nightmare of the lower classes saddened [my] soul."

Something needed to be done, Nicola felt, and anarchism was the answer. It put human beings before the goals of corporations. It encouraged people to care for each other, without having to rely on the government for help that never seemed to come. In an anarchist society, there would be no police, no politicians, no judges, no bosses, no authority; the workers would own everything and distribute wealth according to their needs.

Within two years of the Triangle factory fire, Nicola made anarchism his lifelong mission—more important than anything else, including family. He marched in picket lines and demonstrations, supporting all anarchist groups, even those that resorted to violence—although he never took part in any such actions.

He and Rosina did what they could to help striking workers. They performed in local theatrical productions to raise funds for political prisoners and jailed strikers. One play, *The Martyrs of Chicago*, was about the Haymarket tragedy of 1886, a labor protest that turned into a riot when somebody threw a bomb at the police. Eight anarchists were convicted of murder and four were executed, despite there being no hard evidence against them.

Like those four "martyrs," Nicola vowed to continue fighting for equality and justice.

Bartolomeo was drawn to anarchism for similar reasons. Now that he'd seen America, he knew what drove the factories, the industrial centers, and the country's progress. Workers were breaking their backs, spending their days in dangerous coal mines, steel mills, and factories, and still not earning enough to feed their families. Laws existed to protect workers, but they varied from state to state, and little effort went into enforcing them.

For Bartolomeo, anarchism represented "a belief in human freedom and the dignity of man." It was a way to rid the world of the inequalities he'd witnessed in New York City.

Like Nicola, Bartolomeo joined local anarchist groups and supported laborers at demonstrations and protests. When his former coworkers at the Plymouth cordage factory went on strike in 1916, Bartolomeo actively participated, delivering speeches, walking picket lines, and collecting donations to help the striking workers. He even wrote about the strike in *Cronaca Sovversiva*.

For years, Nicola and Bartolomeo lived about sixty miles from each other. They traveled in the same sphere and took part in the same activities. But it wasn't until May 1917, a month after President Wilson made his fateful decision to enter the war, that they got to know each other. Gathering with other anarchists at a Galleanist meeting in Boston, they surely discussed the draft—how all able-bodied males between the ages of twenty-one and thirty were required to register for military service—and how Galleani had urged his followers to disobey the mandate and flee to Mexico.

Anybody who fought for America, Galleani had warned, would be just like "the soldier who prostitutes himself, the voter who sells out, the servant who adores his chains and kisses the hand that whips him."

To Nicola and Bartolomeo, Galleani made sense. Nicola worked with men of different nationalities and felt kindly toward them. What had they ever done to prompt his waging a battle against their homelands? Bartolomeo had similar misgivings. He couldn't accept that only the poor, and not the wealthy, had to spill their blood on the battlefield. Each man decided on his own to follow Galleani's advice, even though it meant leaving America, their friends, and their homes—and in Nicola's case, his family.

A week after Nicola and Bartolomeo met, they found themselves sitting together on a train, rolling through the Midwest and down into Texas, where along with sixty other Galleanists they crossed the border and settled in Monterrey, Mexico. The anarchists rented adobe houses, taking whatever jobs they could find. Struggling through the insufferably hot Mexican summer, they shared what little they had and developed a brotherhood.

By many accounts, Nicola and Bartolomeo had an even grander vision, one that went beyond simply boycotting America's capitalist war. They had romantic notions about going back to Europe, where Russian workers had revolted against Czar Nicholas II. Galleani had predicted this very thing, insisting that Russia's uprising against an all-powerful government would spread to Italy and other European countries. If it did, Nicola and Bartolomeo wanted to join the fight and promote Galleani's gospel.

But their plans changed when, by the end of summer, the workers' revolution had failed to flourish beyond Russia. Plus, Nicola was tired of life as a refugee. He couldn't speak Spanish, had a hard time adjusting to the food, and failed to land a job as a skilled shoemaker. And he was desperately homesick for Rosina and Dante.

Bartolomeo, too, struggled in Mexico. He kept his long, droopy mustache but shaved off his beard. He found work as a baker—his original job in Italy—and brought home bread for his comrades. But the work was unsatisfying, and he spent much of his time with his books, studying American history, the French Revolution, and the teachings of the German philosopher Karl Marx.

While in exile, Nicola and Bartolomeo kept close tabs on events up north, especially the American government's persecution of Galleanists. Officials had banned *Cronaca Sovversiva* from the mail and arrested Galleani for conspiracy to obstruct the draft.

The anarchists who'd fled the United States had a decision to make: stay in Mexico and avoid the war or return to America and risk being arrested and deported.

Nicola made up his mind to go home to his family.

Bartolomeo, no longer afraid of being forced to fight in the war, also decided to take his chances in America.

And so they both reentered the country, but at that point each went his separate way: Nicola returned to Massachusetts, and Bartolomeo continued wandering, this time to the Midwest.

But going back to the United States wasn't as simple as leaving had been. Both knew that as radicals, as Galleanists, as Italians who had ducked the draft, they and their associates would be watched by the authorities. Federal agents had already shown up at the Brini home in Massachusetts, looking for Bartolomeo's anarchist literature or any other evidence of his radical activities. They'd come within inches of spotting a letter he'd written from Mexico when one of the Brini children grabbed it from the kitchen shelf and hid it in her blouse.

To stay under the radar in Mexico, the two had assumed aliases. Nicola had become Nicola Mosmacotelli, and he kept this name until the war ended in 1918. Bartolomeo was Bartolomeo Negrini, and he, too, kept his fake name until the cease-fire.

What neither of them realized was that the consequences of their activities—attending pro-Galleani meetings, fleeing to Mexico, changing their names—would come back to haunt them.

But they'd soon find out.

Bartolomeo to his family (translated from Italian), from Monterrey, Mexico

July 26, 1917

Dear Father, Dearest Sisters and Brother,

My pen cannot describe these last two months in Mexico. It has been plans, hopes, uncertainties and trepidations . . . However, when I'm established, I will try to describe it all.

Don't respond to this letter because although I intend to stay a little longer here, I will cross the border back to the United States when I am sure it is safe to do so . . . I can always go back whenever I want, having people there who love me and help me.

I am in good health; Mexico has taught me more than a hundred books. When you think of me, you must be calm and content, for life here in forgotten Mexico is as safe as in other places.

Give my best to friends, relatives, and neighbors.

Accept, dear father, many kisses from your son,

Bartolomeo

3

Panic

On April 29, 1919, Ethel Williams, a housekeeper, was working at the home of former Georgia senator Thomas Hardwick. When the morning mail arrived, she found a parcel marked "Gimbel Brothers, 32nd and Broadway, New York City." She opened the box from the department store, expecting to find a set of pencils. But in unsealing the package, she triggered a bomb that instantly tore off both of her hands and blinded her in one eye.

Within days, authorities tracked down twenty-nine identical packages on their way to private citizens, prominent congressmen, governors, mayors, and other officials who, like Hardwick, opposed immigration. Among those targeted were U.S. Postmaster General Albert Burleson, who banned anarchist papers from the mail, and Supreme Court Justice Oliver Wendell Holmes, who had upheld convictions of radicals. Sixteen more packages, each measuring seven inches long and three inches wide, were found sitting in the main post office in Manhattan, their journeys cut short due to insufficient postage.

The United States Department of Justice immediately suspected anarchists, and the country's newspaper editors splashed chilling headlines across their front pages.

MORE BOMBS NOW IN MAILS
New York Evening World

NATION-WIDE NET SPREAD FOR 'RED' LEADERS
Washington Times

MAY DAY DYNAMITE PLOT STARTLES ENTIRE NATION
Reno Evening Gazette

By now, the Great War was over, and millions of soldiers were back home in America. But instead of being at peace, the country was in a full-blown panic. The 1918 influenza pandemic was coursing around the globe, on its way to killing fifty million people—more than half a million of them Americans.

And the United States still feared radicals.

Since a workers' group known as the Bolsheviks gained control during the Russian Revolution, American authorities worried that a similar rebellion could happen in the United States. The Bolsheviks, whose supporters were known as the Reds, were communists—they wanted to eliminate all private ownership and have workers' councils govern the country. So far, their revolution had not spread to the rest of Europe, but what would stop radicals from trying the same thing here?

So, when Nicola and Bartolomeo returned from Mexico in the fall of 1917, they found an America far different from the one they'd left a few months earlier. The government had been stoking the public's fears, railing against immigrants, spreading the word that foreigners were bringing the Bolsheviks' ideas to America. This panic, the Red Scare, took hold of the country. And while the propaganda targeted communists, it also included anarchists, foreigners, or anybody who didn't toe the American line. After all, President Wilson had said back in his annual message to Congress in 1915 that foreigners had "poured the poison of disloyalty into the very arteries of our national life."

America, in essence, had declared war on radicals.

The radicals reciprocated by declaring war on the government.

The first blow had been the bomb that exploded in Ethel Williams's hands. The next one came on Monday night, June 2, 1919. That's when a tall, youngish man strode up R Street Northwest in Washington, D.C., passing a row of stately brick town houses. Dressed in a pin-striped suit, polka-dot tie, and black derby, he headed toward house number 2132, the home of Attorney General A. Mitchell Palmer and his wife, Roberta. Under his arm was a suitcase containing a pile of pamphlets, an Italian-English dictionary, two handguns, and twenty pounds of dynamite.

Palmer, a former congressman who'd turned down the position of secretary of war due to his pacifist Quaker beliefs, was inside his house, getting ready for bed. He turned out the lights in the first-floor library and was heading upstairs when he heard a crash at his front door. Before he could react, a deafening explosion blew open the entire entryway of his home. The eruption shattered windows up and down the block, and panic-stricken residents ran into the street in their pajamas, shouting questions, desperate for answers.

These Washingtonians had no way of knowing that similar

scenes were playing out in other major cities. Bombs exploded in Philadelphia, Cleveland, Pittsburgh, Boston, and New York, as well as Paterson, New Jersey, and Newtonville, Massachusetts. As was the case in D.C., the targets were those who were viewed as anti-radical or anti-anarchist. All escaped serious injury, except for a night watchman in New York City named William Boehner, who was blown up while patrolling the block of a county judge.

Across the street from Palmer's house in Washington, D.C., future president Franklin D. Roosevelt had just arrived home with his wife, Eleanor. He ran to Palmer's aid and found the attorney general rattled but in one piece.

"Everything is all right," Palmer told Roosevelt. "Nobody hurt."

Palmer was only partially correct. He and his wife and daughter had indeed escaped injury, but the explosion had claimed a life. The bomber—the tall man in the derby—had accidentally blown himself up. Investigators sifted through the few bits of forensic evidence left behind, looking for clues that could help them identify the body or lead them to the group behind the bombing.

They found dozens of shredded pink pamphlets titled *Plain Words* strewn all over the neighborhood, apparently let loose in the blast. The literature denounced capitalism and the rich, and bore the signature "The Anarchist Fighters." Police also came upon a train ticket stub that had been stamped in Philadelphia, as well as numerous body parts, including a flap of the bomber's scalp, which was covered with thick, wavy dark hair. Authorities pieced together the evidence and figured the bomber was Carlo Valdinoci, a known associate of Luigi Galleani's. The government had tried for years to deport Valdinoci, but he had managed to elude their grasp. Until now.

The bombing of Attorney General Palmer's house steals the front page.

With their suspicions all but confirmed, government officials stepped up their rhetoric.

Senator Lee Overman of North Carolina called for drastic legislation to silence radicals. Senator Thomas Walsh of Montana introduced a bill to fine or imprison anyone displaying the communist flag or distributing literature advocating violence against the government. Senator William King of Utah went so far as to prepare a bill making it a capital offense, incurring the death penalty, to

U.S. Attorney General A. Mitchell Palmer

belong to an organization advocating the overthrow of the government.

Palmer called the bombings "nothing but a lawless attempt of an anarchistic element in the population to terrorize the country." He then made the most decisive move of all. He reorganized the Justice Department and created the Radical Division, giving it a mandate to track any kind of subversive activity. Palmer handed the division reins to a young lawyer named J. Edgar Hoover, the future director of the FBI.

The twenty-four-year-old Hoover took the job with zeal. With the law on his side—anarchists were now subject to expulsion and deportation—the ambitious Hoover wasted no time. He immediately began collecting infor-

Special Assistant J. Edgar Hoover

mation on suspected radicals, putting into action Palmer's plan to drive them out of the country.

On June 24, after months of legal battles, the government finally deported Galleani and eight other anarchists connected to *Cronaca Sovversiva*. As Hoover gained more responsibility, he began building a database of names and organizations that carried the slightest scent of radicalism. Within a few years, he amassed nearly half a million files.

The skirmish was heating up.

And the stakes were getting much, much higher.

■ ■ ■

Crackdown

In New York City, the Russian People's House served as a gathering place to hold meetings, social events, and education classes for Russian citizens. On any given night, a couple hundred people could be found in the building, socializing, studying, and practicing their English.

Such was the scene on November 7, 1919, when a swarm of federal agents and city cops clustered on East 15th Street at Union Square. At nine o'clock in the evening, they barged inside the four-story brownstone, shouting, swinging blackjacks, drawing their guns, and arresting everyone inside.

Why are we being arrested? a teacher asked. *Where are your warrants?*

The answer was a swift punch to the teacher's face, shattering his glasses. The agents then hunted for signs of radical activity, prying open locked drawers, rummaging through files, throwing desks, shattering framed photographs, and pulling up rugs.

They found no weapons.

They found no secret plans.

They found no criminal evidence.

Still convinced they had unearthed a band of Bolsheviks, they herded the Russians out of the building, forcing them down a stairwell lined by a gauntlet of cops who beat them with billy clubs. By the time the prisoners arrived at federal headquarters, thirty-three required medical attention. No apologies were offered.

It wasn't an isolated incident. That same night, federal agents raided Russian centers in nine other cities. They brought in 450 people for questioning and immediately had to release more than half of them.

No governing body questioned the legitimacy of the raids. And nobody seemed to care.

By the time the sun rose, A. Mitchell Palmer was a national hero. Newspapers across the country praised the raids and ran front-page photos of his stern face, which was always clean-shaven and topped by a shock of neatly combed gray hair. Palmer, eyeing the presidency, was encouraged by the groundswell of support. He made a show of sending 199 Russians who'd broken immigration laws to Ellis Island. There, along with fifty other aliens, they were deported to Russia on the *Buford*, a military ship that the media soon nicknamed "the Soviet Ark."

Most Americans, ecstatic that somebody was ridding the country of dangerous radicals, didn't concern themselves with newspaper reports questioning the agents' methods. But the Palmer Raids—as they came to be known despite being largely directed by Hoover—defied not only the law but also common sense. Hoover had cast a net so wide that he wound up arresting thousands of immigrants, but fewer than six hundred were deemed to be radicals.

To maintain public support, Palmer produced propaganda that openly fed readers' misconceptions. Presented as a newspaper page, one piece featured an article urging Americans to guard against the "Bolshevism menace" and printed photos of deported "Communist agitators" below the warning "Men Like These Would Rule You." Palmer also made his case in *Forum* magazine, warning readers that "sharp tongues of revolutionary heat were licking the altars of the churches, leaping into the belfry of the school bell, crawling into the sacred corners of American homes, seeking to replace marriage vows with libertine laws, burning up the foundations of society."

At the start of the new year, on January 2, 1920, Palmer authorized another series of raids, supposedly targeting two communist political parties. Cloaked in the safety of his public relations machine, he ordered federal agents to round up immigrants in thirty-three cities, many of them in New England.

In Lincoln, New Hampshire, they invaded the home of a paper mill employee. When asked to show a warrant, an agent raised his clenched fist. "This is your warrant," he said.

In Boston—again, armed with guns but no warrant—they pulled a sleeping woman from her bed at six in the morning. It turned out she was an American citizen.

In Lynn, Massachusetts, they busted up a meeting of thirty-nine bakers and hauled them all to the police station, only to find out that nearly half were American citizens.

In Newark, New Jersey, they arrested an immigrant simply because he looked like a radical.

Decades later, U.S. Supreme Court Justice William O. Douglas would write that the government's actions represented "one of the most disgraceful raids in our history."

But for immigrants living in New England at the time, especially Italian anarchists, no officials were speaking on their behalf.

For Nicola and Bartolomeo, the heat was getting closer and closer to home.

■ ■ ■

Crazier and Crazier

In 1920, Nicola was once again settled into a comfortable life with Rosina and Dante. Now twenty-eight, he was bringing home as much as eighty dollars a week at the Three K Shoe Company in Stoughton, Massachusetts. He and his family lived next to the factory in a small rented bungalow. Each morning, he'd wake up before dawn to tend to the fruits and vegetables in his garden, a passion from childhood that had never waned.

And he loved being a father.

He and his son had become so inseparable that Dante, now six, would visit him at the factory after school. He'd stand dutifully by Nicola at the edge trimmer, stacking the soles that fell to the floor. At the end of the day, the two would race each other home, joining Rosina just in time for dinner.

But Nicola was still enraged at the injustices around him, as were many low-wage workers. To take some control over their jobs, millions of workers organized into labor unions and negotiated with management as a group. When their demands weren't met, the workers stuck together. In many cases, they walked off their jobs until the two sides reached an agreement.

Nicola had long believed in worker solidarity, and in 1919, the country had seen the theory put into practice. Fed up and furious that postwar working conditions were as bad as ever, more workers went on strike than at any other time in history. One in five walked off their jobs. The list included telephone operators, Broadway actors, shipyard workers, railroad laborers, and many more. The complaints were almost always the same: low wages, unreasonably long hours, and dangerous machinery.

Thirty-five thousand dressmakers in New York City went on strike.

Sixty thousand workers in Seattle joined the picket lines; twenty-four thousand silk weavers in New Jersey followed suit.

Subway employees in Brooklyn refused to work.

Nearly the entire Boston police force did the same.

By the time 1920 had come around, nearly four million people had gone on strike, hobbling two of the country's biggest industries: coal and steel. The government tried to pin the rash of strikes on foreign radicals—or anarchists—labeling anybody associated with the shutdowns a "Red" or a "Commie."

But Nicola knew it wasn't so. All those workers wanted was a fair shake and some dignity, the same kind of life that he was enjoying. This was supposed to be a free country, yet anybody who tried to organize into a union and demand a living wage was assaulted and jailed.

Even more upsetting, the feds had already identified fellow

anarchist Carlo Valdinoci as the D.C. bomber. Now, in March 1920, they picked up another anarchist, Andrea Salsedo, and tortured him for information about his friends. Word was that he hadn't given up any names, although he'd admitted to printing the pink *Plain Words* pamphlets found strewn throughout Attorney General Palmer's neighborhood.

On May 3, newspapers reported that Salsedo had committed suicide by jumping from the fourteenth floor of the building in downtown Manhattan where the Justice Department had been secretly holding him for two months.

Nicola didn't believe it. Bartolomeo said the feds had thrown Salsedo out of that window—or, at the very least, driven him to jump. According to Bartolomeo, who'd known Salsedo from working with him at *Cronaca Sovversiva*, the prisoner had gotten word to him before he died. *I'm in deep trouble*, Salsedo had written in a letter smuggled out of the room where he'd been held. *We all are. Get rid of any radical literature, anything tied to anarchism. More raids are coming.*

The feds were getting crazier and crazier.

Nicola didn't want to risk the life he had built with Rosina and Dante. But he did want to win his war with the government, his fight for anarchism, his battle for a world in which workers could share the fruits of their labor—and live a dignified life.

Nicola had so much to fight for.

And so much to lose.

Louis Post, former assistant secretary of labor, in his
The Deportations Delirium of Nineteen-Twenty

Nothing is clear about that homicide except that Salsedo was lawlessly a prisoner, that he was held incommunicado in a secret prison controlled by detectives of the Department of Justice, that his prison was fourteen stories above the street, and that his body struck the pavement.

4

Puffer's Place

The robbery in South Braintree—the one that left payroll master Frederick Parmenter and security guard Alessandro Berardelli gunned down in cold blood—had the police flummoxed.

The eyewitnesses were of little help because no two people could agree on what they'd seen. Some said there were five bandits; others said six. Some said one of the gunmen wore a cap; others said he hadn't. Some said the driver was a dark-skinned man; others said he was young and fair-haired. There was even a question about the getaway car: Most witnesses said it was a big, boxy Buick, but others weren't so sure.

A break in the case came two days after the robbery. On Saturday afternoon, April 17, 1920, a pair of horseback riders came upon an abandoned car in the woods of West Bridgewater, about fourteen miles from South Braintree. Bridgewater's police chief, Michael Stewart, sent officers to investigate, and what they found piqued his curiosity. The car, a dark blue Buick, had been stripped of its license plates. It also had a bullet hole in the back door—one that bulged outward, indicating that a gun had been fired from inside. There were powder marks on the leather seat, sixty-nine cents in coins on the rear cushion, and alongside the Buick, a set of thinner tire tracks belonging to a smaller car.

Stewart didn't have any significant experience in hard-core detective work. The son of Irish immigrants, he'd been an amateur boxer and shoe worker until joining the police force nine years earlier. Still, he tried putting the puzzle together. Maybe the Buick was the vehicle used in the South Braintree robbery. If so, the killers could have dumped it in the woods and taken off in a smaller getaway car. That would explain the second set of tracks.

A more experienced detective would likely have known to look for harder evidence. But Stewart came up with a theory anyway. The Buick had been found less than two miles from a house known as Puffer's Place—a hideaway for Italian immigrants. There was no reason to connect the Buick to Puffer's Place, but for Stewart, two miles was as close as two inches.

Puffer's Place

On a hunch, he hopped in his police car, drove over to Puffer's Place, and knocked on the door. When it opened, he found himself face-to-face with Mike Boda, who, Stewart would later learn, was a noted anarchist.

For Stewart, the pieces were falling into place. In his mind, the Buick and the house were connected to the robbery—and so was Boda.

Stewart flashed his badge. *Mind if I take a look around?*

Boda, a short, balding man with a bulbous nose and thin black mustache, shrugged. He let Stewart in and agreed to show him the empty shed behind the house.

You own a car? Stewart asked.

Yeah, an Overland.

Where is it?

It's at the Elm Square garage getting repaired. The damned thing is shot. It barely runs.

Stewart examined the ground inside the shed. It looked as though someone had raked it smooth, but in one area, off to the side, he spotted the faint impression of tire tracks.

Those your tire tracks? he asked, pointing at the dirt.

Yeah, they're from the Overland.

Stewart leaned over and took a closer look. There were two sets of tracks, one fat and one skinny.

If you only drive the Overland, how come there are two sets of tracks?

Again, Boda shrugged. *I don't always pull into the shed the same way. Sometimes I drive in straight, sometimes at an angle.*

Stewart headed back to the station, but something still smelled funny. There had been two sets of tracks in the woods. Now there were two sets of tracks here. The Buick, Puffer's Place, and Boda had to be connected somehow.

One can picture Stewart sitting at his desk, running his hands through his thick black hair, trying to connect the dots. Maybe Boda and his gang had driven the Buick into South Braintree, shot the paymaster and the guard, and taken off with the money. And maybe they ditched the Buick in the woods and piled into the Overland to throw off the police. That would explain the loose change in the Buick—they might have dropped it while transferring the loot from one car to the other. Then, having shaken off the cops, they must have driven the Overland here to West Bridgewater and split up the money.

Even Stewart knew the difference between detective work and guesswork. The next morning, he got into his patrol car and headed back to Puffer's Place. He needed to compare the second set of tire tracks near the shed to those of the Buick. But when he knocked on the door, nobody answered. He peeked in the window and saw that the place had been cleaned out. Then he checked the shed, and found that the tire tracks had been wiped away.

In Stewart's mind, these were the actions of a guilty man. And that guilty man was on the lam.

The following day, Stewart went to the Elm Square garage, where Boda said his car was being repaired. Sure enough, the Overland was sitting in the bay.

He stared at the car and connected one last dot, perhaps making his biggest leap of all: If the Overland had been used in the robbery—if it had been the second getaway car—then whoever came to pick it up must have been involved in the South Braintree murders.

Stewart took a puff on his cigar and walked over to the garage owner, Simon Johnson. He held up his badge. *What's the story on that Overland?*

It's a piece of junk, Johnson said. *My brother and I towed it here a while ago. We'll get it going, but it still needs work.*

Stewart was so blinded by his theory that he didn't bother to ask Johnson how long the car had been there. Instead, he said, *Do me a favor. If anybody comes for that car, don't give it to them. Tell them to come back in a few days, and give me a call the minute they leave.* He jotted down his number. *I just want to talk with the guy.*

Johnson agreed, and Stewart left satisfied. Sooner or later, somebody would come for the Overland and Stewart's phone would be ringing.

■ ■ ■

Arrested

Like Nicola, Bartolomeo couldn't accept that his comrade Andrea Salsedo had leaped to his death. It was obvious the government would stop at nothing to crush anarchists. And it was equally clear that Bartolomeo and his associates were in danger.

At some point, they're going to come for us, he told Nicola. *There's going to be more raids, more harassment. We need to keep a low profile. If they tag us as anarchists, they'll ship us back to Italy. Or they'll shoot us. Look where Andrea ended up.*

Nicola agreed. *We've got to do what Andrea told us to. Let's go round up papers, pamphlets, anything tied to anarchism.*

On the morning of May 5, Bartolomeo and Nicola had breakfast together at Nicola's house. Later that day, Mike Boda and Riccardo Orciani showed up and stayed for dinner. While they were there, Boda called the garage and was told the Overland was ready to be picked up. So the four men hatched a plan: They'd split up and meet at nine o'clock that evening at the Elm Square garage. Once Boda paid for the repair work, they'd use the car to collect whatever incriminating evidence they could find and stash it all in the Overland until the Red Scare had passed.

And so they set out for the Elm Square garage, Orciani on his red motorcycle with Boda in the sidecar, Bartolomeo and Nicola going by trolley.

But there was a hiccup. The garage was locked, and so they went to Simon Johnson's house a quarter of a mile away.

At nine o'clock, with Bartolomeo and Nicola watching from across the street, and Orciani standing by the motorcycle, Boda knocked on Johnson's door. Johnson's wife, Ruth, greeted them.

My husband will be right out, she said. *I need to borrow some milk from my neighbor.*

After she left, Bartolomeo and Nicola waited in the still, dark night as Simon Johnson came to the door and spoke with Boda.

The car's fixed, but your registration is expired, he said.

Okay, Boda said. *I'll come back in a day or two.*

The four men left, splitting up again. Boda and Orciani took off on the motorcycle. Bartolomeo and Nicola walked to the trolley stop. At 9:40, they climbed aboard and headed to Brockton. Twenty minutes later, a police officer got on the same streetcar. He seemed to be looking for somebody and zeroed in on the two Italian men.

Bartolomeo shifted in his seat. This was it; this is what he'd warned his friends about. If the cop pegged them as anarchists, they'd be deported to Italy within weeks.

Where have you two been? the cop asked.

Bartolomeo couldn't tell the truth. How could he say they were going to pick up a car so they could hide anarchist literature?

We went to meet a friend, he said.

The cop didn't waste time chitchatting. He immediately arrested Bartolomeo and Nicola as "suspicious characters" and drove them to the Brockton police station. Both men kept quiet in the squad car and at the precinct, even as the cop fired questions at them. Of particular interest to the police seemed to be the gun and shotgun shells found in Bartolomeo's pocket, and the Colt automatic and anarchist propaganda hidden in Nicola's jacket.

When Bridgewater Police Chief Michael Stewart showed up, he launched into his own line of inquiry.

Are you a communist? he asked Nicola.

No.

Anarchist?

No.

Do you believe in this government of ours?

Yes, but there are some things I like different.

Stewart turned to Bartolomeo.

What about you? Are you an anarchist?

I don't know what you mean.

Do you like this government?

Well, I like things a little different.

Do you believe in changing the government by force, if necessary?

No.

Do you subscribe to anarchist literature?

Sometimes I read it.

Bartolomeo continued dodging the truth, as did Nicola. They lied about their political beliefs, their reasons for carrying guns, their reasons for going to the Elm Square garage, and their reasons for meeting Boda and Orciani.

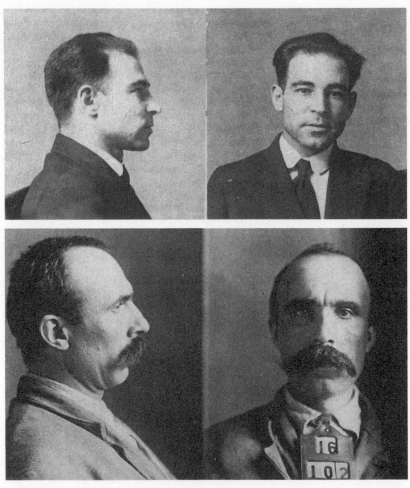

Police photos taken of Nicola and Bartolomeo upon their arrest

After hours of questioning, Nicola and Bartolomeo were locked into empty, squalid cells.

As Bartolomeo stared at the grimy ceiling, a guard walked by, looked in, and spat at him. Then the guard slowly loaded his gun, aimed it at Bartolomeo, and pretended he was about to fire.

Can I have a blanket? Bartolomeo said.

You'll be warm soon enough, the guard said, cryptically. *And in the morning, we'll line you up and shoot you.*

By the time the sun rose, Bartolomeo—unshaven, unwashed, unfed—was terrified. That's when District Attorney Frederick Katzmann arrived at the jail and launched into his own round of questioning.

Did you hear about what happened in South Braintree last month?

Bartolomeo looked at Katzmann's neatly trimmed white hair, his polished nails, his straight, starched collar. This was a powerful man. Why was he here? And where is South Braintree?

Nicola knew little more than Bartolomeo. *I read in the* Boston Post *some bandits robbed people there.*

Where were you that day? Katzmann said

I don't remember, Nicola said. *I think I worked for half the day. I forget.*

Katzmann turned to Bartolomeo. *What about you?*

I can't remember, either.

By the time Katzmann was finished with them, they were charged with carrying concealed weapons and held without bail. It was then that Bartolomeo and Nicola realized they were doomed from the moment they'd shown up at the Johnsons' house. Mrs.

Johnson hadn't gone next door for milk. She'd gone there to call the police and tell them about the four men who had come to pick up the Overland.

Bartolomeo and Nicola had been lying to the police for the wrong reasons.

Nothing about their arrest had to do with anarchism.

It had to do with a robbery in South Braintree.

It had to do with murder.

■ ■ ■

Charged

While Nicola and Bartolomeo were in custody, Attorney General A. Mitchell Palmer's grip on the country finally loosened. Palmer had been warning that radicals were hatching a plot to kill federal and state officials on May 1, 1920, as part of their International Workers' Day celebrations, but his tactics had started to come under scrutiny. Influential lawyers, as well as highly regarded publications like the *Nation* and the *New Republic*, were calling for an end to the unconstitutional actions. It seemed the attorney general's methods were no more legal than they were effective. Assistant Secretary Louis Post, in charge of the Department of Labor and its Immigration Bureau at the time, openly thwarted the attorney general and canceled over two thousand deportation arrest warrants. When the first of May passed without incident, Palmer's support waned.

But that didn't stop the authorities from building a case against Nicola and Bartolomeo.

The police were convinced that Boda was the gang leader behind the South Braintree murders—and that Nicola, Bartolomeo, and Orciani were his partners in crime. But there were two problems. The first was that Boda had vanished in the wind. The second was that Orciani had a rock-solid alibi: He'd been at work when the crime was committed.

That left only two targets: Nicola and Bartolomeo.

The day after arresting them, the cops brought twenty witnesses to the Brockton police station to see whether they could identify the suspects. Playing loose with procedure, they didn't bother with a lineup. They brought each man alone into the middle of a room and asked witnesses if they recognized the person standing in front of them.

One said Bartolomeo looked like the driver of the getaway car in South Braintree. Others didn't recognize him. Some fingered him for a different crime altogether. Back in December, on Christmas Eve 1919, a similar crime, the attempted robbery of a shoe company's payroll, had taken place in the city of Bridgewater. When witnesses said Bartolomeo was the driver of that getaway car, Katzmann pinned both crimes on him—even though Bartolomeo didn't know how to drive.

The Bridgewater case stuck to Bartolomeo like wallpaper paste. On June 11, 1920, the grand jury charged him with attempted robbery. Less than two weeks later, he stood trial, and despite eleven witnesses testifying that they'd seen him working in Plymouth that day—he'd sold them eels for Christmas Eve dinner—the jury convicted him. The judge, Webster Thayer, gave Bartolomeo the maximum sentence of twelve to fifteen years in prison.

Three months later, things got even worse for Nicola and Bartolomeo. On September 11, the grand jury formally charged them with the South Braintree double murder, relying mostly on a statement made about Nicola by a bystander on Pearl Street. "I am pretty positive this man is the man who fired a shot at Berardelli," Lewis Wade said. "I hope I am not mistaken."

Nicola and Bartolomeo were kept in custody without bail, which meant they'd sit behind bars until their case came to trial. Nicola was sent to the Dedham jail. Bartolomeo, having been convicted for the Bridgewater crime, was being held in Charlestown State Prison.

Incarcerated, they had no choice but to wait while the creaky, wobbly wheels of justice ground their way forward.

But the public had no such patience.

On September 16, five days after the grand jury formally charged them with murder, a bomb exploded on Wall Street in New York City just after midday, killing forty people and injuring three hundred others. Standing in the rubble, police and government officials tried to re-create the scene: a horse-drawn wagon loaded with a hundred pounds of dynamite had come to a stop across the street from the J. P. Morgan Building; the driver left the wagon and disappeared into the lunchtime crowd; minutes later, the horse, the wagon, and the street were blown to bits.

There was no hard evidence at the scene, although a stack of leaflets was discovered in a nearby mailbox. Each one read: "Remember, we will not tolerate any longer. Free the political prisoners or it will be sure death for all of you." The message was signed: "American Anarchist Fighters."

That was enough for the police. They immediately suspected the

A man stands over a dead horse after a bomb explodes in front of the J. P. Morgan Building.

bombing was the work of Galleanists in retaliation for the arrests of Nicola and Bartolomeo—but they had no proof. And so no arrests were ever made.

Now government officials were doubly eager to seek vengeance against Galleanists, especially Nicola and Bartolomeo. And so they pushed forward, doggedly pursuing their notion of justice. According to them, the two men were guilty of murder in the first degree; that is, they'd killed Parmenter and Berardelli deliberately, having planned the murder ahead of time. And, in the eyes of the law, it didn't matter if somebody else had pulled the trigger. If Nicola and Bartolomeo had been involved in the killings in any way—even if they'd just been riding in the Buick—then they were as guilty as the gunmen.

If convicted, the two would be sentenced to death.

Bartolomeo to Giovan Battista (translated from Italian), from Charlestown State Prison

October 1, 1920

Dearest Father,

Now they accuse me of murder. I have not killed, nor wounded, nor stolen ever, but if they do as they did in the other trial, they could even find Christ guilty, and they'd already crucified him once.

So be brave, be optimistic. Justice has always triumphed, and it will end up winning this time, too.

Don't hide my arrest. No, don't be silent, I'm innocent and you should not be ashamed. Don't be silent, but shout from the rooftops to everyone of the crime that is being plotted against me.

Every day, nearly the entire Italian press in America stands behind us. Last Sunday, I received a letter in which 200,000 New York workers proclaimed their solidarity, begged me to be of good cheer, and declared their faith in my innocence.

Your son,
Bartolomeo

Nicola, interviewed by Mary Heaton Vorse, in the
magazine *The World Tomorrow*

January 1921

*If I am arrested because of The Idea [anarchism], I am
glad to suffer. If I must I will die for it. But they have arrested
me for gunman job. What have I worked for all my life? I
have worked for educate myself, my comrades. Only so we
go on, by learning . . . Why should they say I do things like
that, when I love all people—my wife, my child, ideas? . . .
Always my wife and I we try help everybody. We give little theatre shows, we get money for strikes. We get money
for all people who need help—not only our own comrades,
Catholics, all people.*

PART TWO

THE TRIAL

1921

5

"Your Goose Is Cooked"

On Memorial Day, May 30, as a heat wave smothered Massachusetts, families gathered in cemeteries across the state. They'd come to honor those who died fighting in the Civil War and the Great War. Schoolchildren topped gravestones with bouquets of flowers. Veteran soldiers, many crippled and battle-scarred, stood at attention, saluting their fallen comrades.

This was America, 1921, and such shows of patriotism were not unusual. It was a time of amped-up rhetoric, of flag-waving propaganda. The Great War had taken more than 116,000 American lives, and an undercurrent of national pride bubbled throughout the country—a prejudice that certainly reached Dedham, the old-money Boston suburb in which Nicola and Bartolomeo were about to be tried for murder.

The following day, in downtown Dedham, the trial of the two anarchists—Nicola and Bartolomeo—was getting under way. Shortly before nine in the morning, a group of armed guards roused Nicola and Bartolomeo from their cells, handcuffed them, and led them to High Street. Nicola, looking gaunt and tired after spending eight months in jail, had on a dark suit and derby. Bartolomeo, whose face had grown old and weary in the many months he'd been behind bars, wore a long coat and sporty cap. Flanked by a cordon of guards, the prisoners climbed the massive stone steps leading into the courthouse. When they arrived in the second-floor courtroom, two guards sat them in an open-topped iron cage, then stood on either side of it.

Nicola's wife, Rosina, sat behind the cage that imprisoned her husband. To keep their children out of the spotlight—Dante was now eight, and a daughter, Ines, had been born several months earlier while Nicola was in jail—Rosina left them in the care of family friends.

The atmosphere in the huge room was half authority and half zoo, with all eyes glued to the two caged animals. The pretrial publicity had only amped up the tension. District Attorney Frederick

Rosina Sacco with infant Ines and Dante

Katzmann, who would lead the prosecution team, had told reporters he'd been targeted by radicals for months, that he and his staff had been vilified, harassed, and threatened. Many Italians, he said, especially those in the North End of Boston, had been spreading word that he was keeping six bottles of champagne in his cellar, saving them to toast the deaths of Nicola and Bartolomeo.

But now, within the thick plaster walls of the courtroom, Katzmann was on his turf. He'd been a prosecutor for eleven years and considered himself a proud son of Massachusetts, having gone to Boston Latin School, Harvard College, and Boston University School of Law. He had a rep-utation for playing within the rules; members of the bar said he wouldn't hit "below the belt, but . . . would give you an hor-rendous going over above it."

Fred Moore, a fiery labor attorney known for represent-ing political radicals, stood opposite Katzmann, ready to lead the defense for Nicola and Bartolomeo. Moore, a dark-haired westerner with bushy

Prosecutor Frederick Katzmann

eyebrows, was an outsider. He had been hired, along with local lawyer Jeremiah McAnarney, by the Sacco-Vanzetti Defense Com-mittee. Formed by Aldino Felicani, an Italian journalist and close friend of Bartolomeo's, the committee had raised $100,000 from donors as far away as Italy. The money was used to pay for the defendants' attorneys, court fees, and expert witnesses—and in Nicola's case, his family's living expenses.

Moore had to wonder if he was fighting an uphill battle. Judge Webster Thayer, sixty-three, was the white-haired ruler of this one-room kingdom. He came from a family of New England Protestants and was known to be a "proud Yankee." As such, he had little use for foreigners in his courtroom. It was common knowledge that he hated Nicola and Bartolomeo for their political views, which was why he'd thrown the book at Bartolomeo for the attempted robbery in Bridgewater.

Defense attorney Fred Moore

Jeremiah McAnarney, fearing that Thayer would eat Moore alive, had suggested replacing him with leading Boston attorney William Thompson. But Moore refused to step down; he was confident that with justice on his side, he could out-lawyer Katzmann, despite the prejudices that infected the minds of so many Americans.

Curious to observe the proceedings for himself, Thompson spent a day sitting in the courtroom. After seeing Thayer

Judge Webster Thayer

repeatedly treat Moore with disdain, Thompson became convinced that this was a case of David versus Goliath—and this particular David didn't have a slingshot hidden in his briefcase.

He shared that assessment with McAnarney.

"Your goose is cooked," he told him.

■ ■ ■

Twelve White Men

Thayer took his seat behind the high desk at the front of the room, his white hair and mustache contrasting with his dark robe. He looked down at the roomful of men summoned for jury duty that day.

As citizens of the commonwealth of Massachusetts, you have a duty to serve, he told the potential jurors in a gravelly voice. *I won't tolerate phony excuses or other attempts to avoid service on this jury.*

Each one listened in silence, but it was clear that no citizens wanted any part of the trial, especially since a guilty verdict meant that the defendants would be put to death.

Of the five hundred men summoned for jury duty, only seven passed the rounds of questions meant to determine their impartiality. Thayer ordered the sheriff to round up two hundred fifty more candidates.

How are we supposed to do that? the sheriff asked. *Everybody in the state knows who we are. They run the minute they see us coming!*

Thayer refused to believe the sheriff could not find twelve acceptable men to sit in judgment of the defendants.

Just find them, he demanded.

And so the sheriff's deputies marched into farmhouses, concert halls, Masonic lodges, even trolley cars, corralling able-bodied men—regardless of the consequences. In one instance, they pulled a man from his wedding dinner. The newlyweds, married for all of four hours, were forced to postpone their honeymoon so that Thayer could question the groom.

One potential juror, shamelessly trying to avoid serving, pretended he'd lost his hearing—a pretense immediately shattered when he had no problem answering the judge's questions.

What is your vocation? Thayer asked.

I'm a sugar dealer, the man answered.

And you're saying you can't serve because . . . ?

I'm deaf, your honor.

Even Nicola and Bartolomeo, inside their cage, burst out laughing, their shoulders shaking while they palmed tears off their cheeks. With his ludicrous response, the sugar dealer had, for the moment, broken the somber atmosphere that hovered over the room.

After four days of interrogating jurors about any biases they might have toward the defendants, the court finally settled on twelve men. The jury, which was meant to represent the defendants' peers, comprised a grocer, a mason, two machinists, a retired police chief, two factory workers, a photographer, a farmer, two real estate agents, and a clothing salesman. Since women were not allowed to serve, and no Black people were chosen, the jury was all white and all male. And all were American-born.

Thayer made no secret as to what he expected. He reminded the jurors that their job wasn't simply to deliver a just verdict but also to protect the American way of life. On the first day of the trial, he hammered them with divisive language about "us" and "them," thus widening the chasm that the Great War had left in its wake.

I expect you to perform with the same spirit of patriotism, courage, and devotion to duty that American soldiers demonstrated on the battlefields of Europe, he told them.

Apparently, the message was received, if not by the entire jury, at least by sixty-nine-year-old Walter H. Ripley, the oldest juror. A former police chief, Ripley was appointed jury foreman. In the days leading up to the trial, he ran into an old friend, William H. Daly, outside the courthouse. When Daly expressed doubts as to the defendants' guilt, Ripley replied: "Damn them, they ought to hang them anyway."

And so the trial of Nicola and Bartolomeo began with the two men locked in an iron cage.

To their left sat a bullheaded district attorney in Katzmann.

On the bench presided a biased judge in Thayer.

And in the jury box loomed a foreman who already felt that, guilty or not, Nicola and Bartolomeo deserved to die.

Bartolomeo to Giovan Battista (translated from Italian), from Charlestown State Prison

May 24, 1921

Dear Father,

Next week, May 31, my second trial begins.

I want you to know that I have a skilled lawyer and a formidable group of generous people supporting me.

By the time you receive this letter, the trial will probably be over, and I hope with it my acquittal.

You can't imagine the present state of this country. It is no longer the America that you admired 30 or more years ago. In fact, the whole world is no longer the world that it once was.

We live in a sad time—a corrupt time, a time in which power is attacked and desperately defends itself.

No one should be surprised by the most improbable events. So, stay calm and confident. History is on our side.

Your son,

Bartolomeo

6

"That Man There"

When Assistant District Attorney Harold Williams delivered his opening remarks, the courtroom was so hot that Judge Thayer told the jurors they could take off their suit jackets and roll up their shirtsleeves. Williams, thirty-eight, a graduate of Harvard Law School, was assisting District Attorney Fred Katzmann on the case. As the prosecutors, Williams and Katzmann had a job to do: convince the jury to convict Nicola and Bartolomeo without hesitation. In other words, to find them guilty beyond a reasonable doubt.

With that in mind, Williams laid out the crime for the jury: how at about three o'clock on the afternoon of April 15, 1920, Frederick Parmenter and Alessandro Berardelli left the Slater & Morrill offices in Hampton House carrying two cashboxes filled with almost $16,000; how two men ambushed them and started shooting; how Berardelli was shot three times, fell to the ground, was shot a fourth time, and died on the street; how Parmenter, shot once, turned to run away, was shot again, and died the next morning in Quincy City Hospital. He told the jury how the two gunmen grabbed the cashboxes, piled into a getaway car, and hightailed it over the railroad tracks and out of South Braintree.

Williams said there were five men in the getaway car but, strangely, never said a word about what had become of them. If Nicola and Bartolomeo were involved, what happened to the other three bandits? Did the police even know who they were? And where was the stolen money? It certainly hadn't been traced to either defendant.

What Williams did explain, however, was the prosecution's theory about the crime, the dots the police had connected, the leaps they'd made.

Nicola Sacco shot and killed Frederick Parmenter and Alessandro Berardelli, he said, his voice ringing with certainty. *Sacco's accomplice, Bartolomeo Vanzetti, sat in the car while the shooting occurred, which, in the eyes of the law, makes him just as guilty as the man who fired the fatal shot.*

Nicola and Bartolomeo could do nothing but sit silently in their cage, hoping the jury would keep an open mind as Williams started to call witnesses. One was Mary Splaine, a bookkeeper at Slater & Morrill who had been working with Parmenter the day he was killed. Williams asked Splaine what she saw after Parmenter left the office—specifically, after she heard gunshots coming from Pearl Street.

"I stood up in the middle of the office," she said. "Then I walked to the window on the south side."

Then what happened?

"I saw an auto as it was approaching about the second track, just about leaving the crossing, come up Pearl Street . . . There was a man appeared on the side of the machine."

A man? What did he look like?

"Slightly taller than I am. He weighed possibly from 140 to 145 pounds . . . I noticed particularly the left hand was a good-sized hand . . . He had a gray, what I thought was a shirt . . . The hair was brushed back and it was between . . . two inches and two-and-one-half inches in length and had dark eyebrows, but the complexion was a white, peculiar white that looked greenish."

Do you see that man in this courtroom?

All heads turned to the iron cage in the center of the room. There, the defendants sat motionless. As Splaine raised her hand and extended her index finger toward Nicola, the air seemed to lose its oxygen and, somehow, get even hotter. Creaking benches and flapping paper fans came to a dead stop. Now the only sound in the room was the incessant ticking of the clock on the wall.

"The man sitting . . . over there," Splaine said. "What do you call it, a cage?"

The man with the mustache? Or without?

"The man without the mustache."

Do you know his name?

"Well, I have learned it since."

What name did you learn?

"Nicola Sacco."

The spectators murmured and fixed their stares on Nicola. In their eyes, the bookkeeper had just pegged him, without question, as the gunman hanging from the side of the Buick.

But defense attorney Fred Moore saw things differently. When his time came to cross-examine Splaine, he ran his hand through his dark hair and walked toward the witness box. He could accept that she had seen a car speeding from the crime scene, but how could she have possibly identified someone inside it with such detail? Besides, she'd given a different story back in May.

Do you remember testifying in a preliminary hearing a few weeks after the crime, Miss Splaine? You said then you could have been mistaken about the man you saw. Isn't that correct?

"No, I did not say that."

I will read back your original statement. You said, "I will not swear positively he is the man."

"I did not answer that question that way."

Hmm. Okay, let's talk about today. When you were speaking with Assistant District Attorney Williams, you said the man wore a gray shirt. What kind of shoulders do you say the man had?

"They were straight out, square, well, like yours."

His height?

"Well, I should think he was a little taller than I am."

Weight?

"I should think perhaps 145 pounds."

And you saw all this from eighty feet away? And you'd never seen the man before?

"Not to my knowledge."

Jeremiah McAnarney was surely thinking the same thing as Moore: Splaine was changing her description now that she was getting a good look at Nicola. McAnarney took over for Moore, focusing his questions on the description Splaine had given—and bungled badly—before the trial.

Do you remember, a week after the murders, going to the police station and looking at photos of different men? You pointed at one and said, with certainty, that he had the features of the man who leaned out of the getaway car.

"They were a striking resemblance to the man."

Do you also remember that the man you identified was in prison at the time?

"I learned the man was not at large."

Do you recall telling the police you weren't in a position to identify the man?

"Yes."

Was that the truth?

"Yes, sir."

Thank you, Miss Splaine. That's all.

Satisfied that he had cast enough doubt on Splaine's testimony, McAnarney had no more questions.

But Katzmann still had a long list of witnesses. He called Louis Pelser, a shoe cutter who'd been working at the Rice & Hutchins factory on Pearl Street when the crime occurred. Pelser seemed nervous right from the start. As he explained what he'd seen, sweat rolled down his forehead onto his ears and neck.

Pelser testified that he'd heard three gunshots outside the factory, peeked through the window, and saw Berardelli lying motionless on the ground. He opened the window and saw the shooter empty his gun into the fallen security guard.

When asked if he saw the shooter in the courtroom, Pelser answered, "Well, I wouldn't say it was him, but he is a dead image of him."

Asked to identify the man, Pelser pointed toward the cage and said, "Right in the cage on the right-hand side. Not the fellow with the mustache."

He was pointing at Nicola Sacco.

Fred Moore dug further into the story. As he did so, the

eyewitness started fidgeting even more, shifting from one foot to the other. If body language was any indication, Pelser was terrified that his story wouldn't stand up under scrutiny.

The windows in that building are opaque, aren't they? Moore asked. *That is, you can't see through them?*

"Yes, sir. You can't see through the window."

So, when the shooting started, what could you see?

"Well, there was a little window open about that much," Pelser said, using his thumb and forefinger to indicate a span of a few inches.

And your statement to the jury is that, through that small crack, you saw a body lying on the ground?

"Yes, sir . . . he was lying right in the middle of the sidewalk."

And that was the body of Mr. Berardelli?

"Yes, sir."

Now, did you see any shooting at that time?

"When I opened the window, I seen him shooting."

How long did you stay at the window?

"I would say about a minute."

Mr. Pelser, a few months ago, one of our investigators, Mr. Reid, spoke with you about the case, correct?

"Yes, sir."

And you told him freely and frankly everything that you knew about this case?

"Not everything, no, sir," Pelser said as he tugged on the lapels and cuffs of his dark suit.

You didn't speak freely and frankly?

"I told him some, but I didn't tell him the whole story."

In other words, part of the things you told him were true?

"Yes, sir."

You said you only saw the body on the ground. That is a correct statement of what you told Mr. Reid?

"That I told Mr. Reid, yes, sir."

Was that the truth?

"No, sir."

You also said you hadn't seen the shooter because you'd ducked under a bench inside the factory. Is that correct?

"Yes, sir."

So you ducked under the bench?

"No, sir."

Pelser wasn't making any sense, and he seemed to know it. His eyes shifted from Thayer, to the guards, and back to Moore, as though he expected them to throw him into the cage alongside Nicola and Bartolomeo.

Didn't you just finish telling Mr. Williams that you were scared?

"Yes, sir."

So you ducked under the bench during the shooting. Is that right?

"Yes, sir."

Why didn't you tell that to the jury half a second ago?

"Well, I didn't."

By the time Pelser stepped out of the witness box, his lips were trembling and his skin had turned a sickly green hue.

The prosecutors, Katzmann and Williams, continued to call witnesses, including Lola Andrews, a passerby in South Braintree on the day of the crime. Andrews testified that she had just applied for a job at Slater & Morrill when she met up with two men near a shiny Buick, one of whom was working underneath the car. She asked the man tinkering with the car for directions and, supposedly, got a good look at his face.

At the trial, she took the stand wearing a black straw hat and flowered dress—appearing surprisingly fresh, considering the air was still moist and heavy.

Assistant District Attorney Williams started the questioning.

The man who was working on the car—do you see him in the courtroom now?

"I think I do, yes, sir," she said, pointing toward the cage, directly at Nicola. "That man there."

Nicola leaped to his feet and shouted at Andrews.

"I am the man?" He jerked his thumb toward his face, which, as the days wore on, had been getting paler, thinner, and bonier. "Do you mean me? Take a good look."

The spectators put down their fans and chattered to one another.

An armed guard shoved Nicola back into his seat, but Nicola continued glaring at Andrews, beads of sweat soaking his neck and stiff collar.

Andrews continued testifying, but the exchange with Nicola seemed to break her composure. She was now visibly nervous, pulling at her hair and more than once running out of the room, insisting she needed a break. On the second day of her testimony, she began to unravel. She had been under cross-examination all morning, and when she returned to the stand after lunch, Judge Thayer told her she could sit down. She said it wasn't necessary, but moments later, her face drained of color. Katzmann ran over to her just as she fainted, her knees buckling, her body plopping into the district attorney's arms.

Immediately after Andrews collapsed, a male spectator got up and left the room. Then a deputy sheriff escorted two other men into the hallway. Thayer, from the bench, ordered the room locked down. Court officers closed the doors and guarded the entrance.

Thayer offered no explanation and ordered the trial to resume.

Lola Andrews makes headlines in Boston.

The next witness was Michael Levangie, the gatekeeper who'd been working at the railroad crossing when the bandits sped out of South Braintree. His testimony would be critical to the prosecution's case because he claimed to have seen Bartolomeo during the getaway.

On the witness stand, he said he spotted an automobile coming up the hill.

"The first thing I knew, there was a revolver pointed like that at my head. I looked back at the train to see if I had a chance enough to let them go. I saw there was chance . . . and I let them."

Despite going on to say that the car was dark and covered in dust—and was moving nearly twenty miles an hour—Levangie claimed he could identify the driver.

He was a "dark complected man, with cheek bones sticking out, black hair, heavy brown mustache, slouch hat, and army coat," he said, describing Bartolomeo, who was sitting right in front of him.

When Fred Moore approached Levangie to ask his own questions on cross-examination, he strode in front of the witness box, slowly, holding his chin, mulling over the statements the guard had just made.

Mr. Levangie, do you remember describing the man you saw as light-skinned? Say, a Swedish or Norwegian type of person?

"No, sir. The man that I saw was dark complected."

Moore tried again to get Levangie to recall how he'd previously described Bartolomeo, but the gatekeeper stuck to his answer. At that point, Moore said he had no more questions and the prosecution moved on to its next witnesses.

The following day, Williams called Frances Devlin, who worked as a bookkeeper at Slater & Morrill. Like Louis Pelser, she identified Nicola as the South Braintree shooter.

But when he cross-examined Devlin, McAnarney pointed out that her description of the killer—a good-sized man, fairly tall—in no way resembled Nicola's physique. At five-foot-six, he was neither good-sized nor fairly tall. For that matter, Devlin's assertion that the man had a "white complexion" also rang false, since Nicola's skin was olive-colored. As a final blow, McAnarney had Devlin, like fellow bookkeeper Mary Splaine, admit that she'd already told the police she wasn't sure that Nicola was the right man.

If either Katzmann or Williams was worried that their theory was being discredited, they showed no such concern. They simply called more witnesses, perhaps hoping that the quantity of testimony, if not its truthfulness, would persuade the jury.

To address the issue of Nicola's pistol, Katzmann turned to veteran ballistics expert William H. Proctor of the Massachusetts State Police.

It was generally accepted that the fatal bullet, the one that killed Berardelli, had been fired from a .32-caliber Colt, the same type of weapon carried by Nicola—along with two hundred thousand other gun owners. Calling Proctor was a risky move, because he had already tested the bullet and found no evidence that it had been fired by Nicola's gun. But that didn't deter Katzmann.

Captain Proctor, do you have an opinion as to whether the fatal bullet—bullet number four—came from Sacco's Colt automatic?

"I have."

What is it?

"That the appearance of it is consistent with having been fired from that gun."

It was a damning statement, and Katzmann was surely happy

with it. On June 21, a little more than three weeks after the trial had started, the prosecution rested its case.

It was now time for the defense team to call its own witnesses, three of whom directly refuted Michael Levangie's testimony. The first, a shoe worker at Slater & Morrill, said that Levangie had told him the getaway driver was "light-complected," not dark. The second, a freight clerk for the railroad, testified that about fifteen minutes after the shooting he overheard Levangie saying "it would be hard to identify" the men in the car. The third, a locomotive fireman, said that after the shooting Levangie had told him he was so scared that he had run for cover.

The defense team continued trying to poke holes in the prosecution's case. In so doing, it called to the stand three of Louis Pelser's coworkers. All three testified that Pelser had never gone to the window at all. In fact, it was one of his coworkers, Peter McCullum, who had opened the window and then shut it right away, yelling "Duck!" Everybody in that part of the factory, including Pelser, had done whatever they could to avoid being hit by a stray bullet. In Pelser's case, they said, he'd taken cover under a bench.

To discredit Lola Andrews's testimony, McAnarney called her friend Julia Campbell to the stand. The sixty-nine-year-old Campbell had been job-hunting with Andrews on the day in question; she agreed that they'd walked out of the Slater & Morrill factory and passed two men near a shiny Buick. But, according to Campbell, Andrews had never spoken to the man who was working underneath the car, and neither of them had seen anyone resembling Nicola or Bartolomeo that day.

During cross-examination, Katzmann tried his best to shake Campbell's recollection, but she never wavered.

"I do not think I ever saw them men in the world," she said.

McAnarney wasn't done disproving Andrews's testimony. In addition to Campbell, he called Harry Kurlansky to the stand. According to Kurlansky, who owned a business on Andrews's block, Andrews had complained to him that the government had been "bothering" her to identify the defendants. Kurlansky told the court that he could clearly remember Andrews telling him, "I don't know a thing about them. I have never seen them and I can't recognize them."

To raise doubt about Captain Proctor's testimony, McAnarney brought in his own ballistics expert, who said he could find no evidence connecting the bullet that killed Berardelli to Nicola's Colt—or, for that matter, to any Colt. According to the defense expert, the fatal bullet could have been fired from a Belgian gun called a Bayard.

At this point in the trial, it seemed the defense team had successfully planted "reasonable doubt" in the minds of the jury. The prosecution's witnesses had failed to positively identify the defendants as the murderers, and its ballistics expert had been unconvincing.

But the trial wasn't over.

Bartolomeo to Giovan Battista (translated from Italian), from Charlestown State Prison

June 1921

Dearest Father,

I know you sent a telegram asking about the outcome of the trial. It still isn't over. Our lawyers think it will end in a week or two.

Things seem to be going well. And I'm certain that before this letter reaches you, the trial will be over and you will already know the outcome. So, the main reason for this letter is to inform you of my excellent health and state of mind and to pray that you take care of your health, and don't let my misfortune destroy you.

However this trial ends, my innocence remains . . . Truth and justice will prevail; the people are with me.

So, have faith that we will soon see each other again.

Best wishes and kisses from your son,

Bartolomeo

7

Alibis

The jurors were getting restless. They'd been sitting through weeks and weeks of testimony—the prosecution alone having called fifty-nine witnesses—and defense attorney Fred Moore was still going at it. He had already lined up dozens of witnesses, including those who said they had been within inches of the shooting. All had agreed with absolute certainty that the bandits bore no resemblance to either defendant.

Operating on the theory that no human being could be in two places at the same time, Moore was now introducing witnesses who'd seen Nicola on that fateful day—nowhere near South Braintree. They'd spotted him many times in downtown Boston: at a restaurant, a coffee shop, a produce stand, the train station, and the Italian consulate.

A clerk who was working at the consulate, Giuseppe Adrower, had returned to Italy but gave his testimony from Rome so it could be read to the jury. According to Adrower, Nicola had been at the consulate when the crime was taking place. He remembered Nicola bringing in a passport photo that was too big. Adrower had told him to come back with a smaller one; he even produced a record of Nicola's payment of fifteen dollars.

Rosina Sacco speaks with Bartolomeo (left) and Nicola during the trial.

When it came to Bartolomeo's whereabouts, several people testified that they'd seen him in the town of Plymouth—nearly thirty miles from the scene of the crime. Alfonsina Brini, Bartolomeo's friend and former landlady, told the court she'd met with Bartolomeo and a clothing peddler, Joseph Rosen. The two men had brought her some cloth, she said, hoping she could help Bartolomeo pick out fabric for a new suit. Rosen told the same story, adding that he was sure of the time because he'd heard the noon whistle coming from the Plymouth cordage factory. Other residents agreed, insisting Bartolomeo had been in Plymouth, selling them fish later that same day.

One witness, a truck driver, even said he'd heard the police chief, Michael Stewart, tell a fellow officer at the Brockton police station, "We haven't got the right men."

But Katzmann didn't accept the testimonies without a fight. He bombarded the witnesses with questions, deliberately trying to confuse them—and prove that their memories were not as sharp as they claimed.

One witness recalled being with Nicola in Boston around three o'clock on the day of the shooting. The man said he remembered the day because he'd gone to a banquet that night. But, upon cross-examination, Katzmann fired more than eighty questions at him, mocking him, showing that it was impossible to remember where he was at three o'clock on any given day, let alone on April 15.

Was there anybody with you at three o'clock the day after the banquet? How about the day after that? Or the day after that? Do you remember anything at all? Okay, how about twenty-two days ago? What were you doing at three o'clock? Twenty-one days ago? Twenty days ago?

Katzmann was putting on a show, and to onlookers in the courtroom, it seemed to work. The jurors were laughing, even elbowing each other in admiration of his theatrics.

Apparently, for the moment, they'd forgotten that two men's lives were at stake.

■ ■ ■

Bartolomeo Takes the Stand

On July 5, the defense called Bartolomeo to the stand. The court had taken a three-day break for Independence Day, but the heat wave continued to stifle New England. Sweltering temperatures had already sent seventeen local residents to the hospital with heatstroke and were still sucking the air out of the courtroom. Only Judge Thayer had any relief. On his desk, an electric fan buzzed, sending a warm breeze in his, and only his, direction.

In the witness box, Bartolomeo stood erect, his chin up, as beads of sweat rolled past his angular cheekbones, moistening his bushy mustache. Answering McAnarney's questions, he recounted,

Jurors relax during the Fourth of July holiday.

step by step, what he was doing on April 15—an explanation that matched, identically, the testimonies given by Alfonsina Brini, Joseph Rosen, and others. He'd sold fish in the morning. He'd looked at suit fabric that Rosen was selling around noon. Then he'd gone to Alfonsina's house to show her the material. After that, he said, he'd spent more than an hour at the shore visiting with his friend Melvin Corl, a fisherman who was painting his boat. At the end of the day, he brought his fish cart home, changed his clothes, and ate dinner.

When Katzmann got up to cross-examine Bartolomeo, he didn't start by reviewing his account of the day in question. Instead, he hammered Bartolomeo about his political views. It was a calculated move, since the two defendants had already admitted to being anarchists—and most Americans, including Judge Thayer, wouldn't give a radical leftist the wet end of a chewed cigar.

So, Mr. Vanzetti, in May 1917, you left Plymouth to dodge the draft. Is that correct?

Before Bartolomeo could answer, Katzmann went at him again.

You deserted America so you wouldn't have to fight as a soldier? Is that true?

As soon as Bartolomeo tried to explain himself—under fire, in halting English—it was apparent that the self-educated thirty-three-year-old immigrant was no match for the seasoned attorney.

"I don't refuse because I don't like this country or I don't like the people of this country," he said. "I will refuse even if I was in Italy, and you tell me it is a long time I am in this country and I tell you that in this country as long time as I am, that I found plenty good people and some bad people."

It was Judge Thayer's role to keep lawyers and witnesses on track, to make sure they didn't stray from the facts. But Katzmann's interrogation about Bartolomeo's politics went unchecked by Thayer, so the district attorney continued barking out questions that had nothing to do with South Braintree, Frederick Parmenter, or Alessandro Berardelli.

Katzmann fired his questions so quickly that the defendant struggled to follow along. At one point, Bartolomeo asked for a glass of water and drank it thirstily, wiping his mustache with the back of his hand when he was finished.

Let's turn our attention to May fifth, Katzmann said in a harsh tone. *Did you hide radical literature at Sacco's house?*

"No."

Did Sacco?

"I don't know."

Did you talk about hiding it?

"Yes."

But you didn't?

"No, we had no means."

So you did? Or you didn't? Answer my questions! Answer them directly!

After practically accusing Bartolomeo of being up to no good on the night he was arrested, Katzmann turned to Bartolomeo's alibi.

Whom did you sell fish to that day? Do you remember? What are their names? List the names. I want to know every name. Tell me right now, unless you can't remember. You said you knew, and now you don't? Which is it?

"I make a mistake," Bartolomeo said, palming sweat from his neck. "Not meant for a liar, but a mistake that I don't remember exactly the particulars, and the number of minutes, the number of the steps I made."

When Bartolomeo left the witness box, he was sweaty, shaken, and no doubt upset that he'd done so poorly when answering questions about his political beliefs. And why did it matter, anyway? The trial was supposed to be about the murders of two people in South Braintree.

■ ■ ■

Nicola in the Witness Box

The following day, July 6, Nicola took the stand. He was no longer the robust, healthy-looking man who used to race Dante home from the Three K Shoe Company factory. Only thirty years old, Nicola had taken on the look of the imprisoned: gaunt, frail, and jittery.

On the stand, he went through his whereabouts on the day of the crime. He'd spent much of the day in downtown Boston, first at Boni's Restaurant, where he had lunch with a friend, Felice Guadagni. Then he'd gone to the Italian consulate and dealt with the passport clerk, Giuseppe Adrower. On his way back to the train station, he'd stopped at Giordani's coffeehouse and then at the fruit peddler Carlos Affe, where he paid an overdue bill of $15.67. Finally, he boarded the 4:12 train to Stoughton and arrived home at six o'clock.

Instead of launching into an attack on Nicola's politics, Katzmann aimed to prove that Nicola had shown a "consciousness of guilt"—that is, he'd acted guilty—on the night he was arrested. He'd lied to the police, as had Bartolomeo. Why hide the truth if you're innocent?

Nicola was easy prey for the bullish Katzmann, especially since he, like Bartolomeo, struggled with English. Perhaps afraid to let somebody else speak for him, he'd rejected the help of a translator. But he was now clearly confused by the questions, and was bungling his answers.

Do you remember my asking you if you knew Mike Boda?
"Yes."
Do you remember saying, "No, sir, I never heard of him"?

"Yes, sir."

Were those answers true or false?

"False."

What was your reason?

"If I did say I knew Mike Boda, and I know he is a radical, I am a radical, that is the question I been trying to keep behind."

Do you remember my asking you where you were on the night of May fifth last year? You told me "About half-past or quarter-past six we started to walk towards the railroad to meet a car come from Stoughton." Did you say that?

"Yes."

Is that true?

"No, that is not true."

Why did you tell me a falsehood?

"I did not get my mind to remember."

Do you remember my asking you how long you knew Bartolomeo Vanzetti? And you said nearly two years. Was that true?

"It was not true."

What was the sense in telling a falsehood?

"Because I do not remember."

Katzmann then did to Nicola what he had done to Bartolomeo: attack his unpatriotic and despised beliefs.

Mr. Sacco, didn't you say yesterday you love this country? Did you love it in May 1917, when you went to Mexico to avoid serving in the war? When you deserted your country—and ran away from your wife?

"I did not run away from her."

Don't you think abandoning your country is a vulgar thing to do when she needs you?

"I don't believe in war."

Do you think it is a cowardly thing to do what you did?

"Yes, sir."

Do you think it would be a brave thing to go away from your own wife?

"No."

When she needed you?

"No."

But you left, anyway. Is that your idea of showing your love for your country? And for your wife?

Katzmann drilled Nicola with more than a hundred questions. And no matter how many times Fred Moore raised an objection, Judge Thayer allowed Katzmann to roam freely, seemingly without any boundaries.

Realizing that he wasn't keeping up with Katzmann—and that he was hurting instead of helping his own cause—Nicola finally relented and asked Judge Thayer for an interpreter.

"Excuse me, I like to say, Judge, to get the interpreter," he said. "I have been thinking, I did make some mistake. I understand wrong."

The court obliged, but having an interpreter couldn't undo the damage. Nicola wasn't able to erase what he'd already said, nor was he able to extinguish the fire known as District Attorney Katzmann.

After three days of unrelenting questions, Nicola finished his testimony, dark crescents having formed under his eyes, the blood having drained from his lips.

■ ■ ■

A Dilemma

The trial was nearing its conclusion; all that was left was for the two sides to deliver their final remarks to the jury.

Fred Moore felt that Bartolomeo had a solid case. The prosecution had presented virtually no evidence against him. Thirty-one witnesses had testified that he was not in the getaway car; thirteen others had said he was in Plymouth selling fish on the day of the murders.

Moore gave him a choice.

I'm guessing the jury will find you innocent, he said. *But I doubt they'll find both of you innocent. If I push for the jury to free you, they will likely convict Nicola. What should I do?*

Bartolomeo didn't need time to think about his answer.

"Save Nick," he said. "He has the woman and the child."

■ ■ ■

Waiting

On Sunday, July 10, the heat wave in New England finally broke.

In its place came a violent electrical thunderstorm that dumped more than six inches of rain on Dedham. It toppled trees, split church steeples in half, washed out bridges and tunnels, shut down telephone and telegraph systems, and suspended train service between Boston and New York.

Judge Thayer spent the day at his private country club in Worcester. Supposedly, during the trial, he had told a fellow member of his disdain for Nicola and Bartolomeo. He called them "those bastards down there" and swore he'd "get them good and proper," vowing to see them hanged.

While Thayer was mingling with his friends, Nicola and Bartolomeo sat in their cells, alone. Their only hope was that the defense team could convince a jury of patriotic white men that they were nowhere near South Braintree on the day Frederick Parmenter and Alessandro Berardelli were murdered in cold blood.

Frank P. Sibley in the *Boston Globe*, "Sacco Faces Sharp Grilling on Murder"

July 8, 1921

The courtroom was more crowded than it has been on any day in the six weeks the trial has been going on . . . The day has been so hot and moist that the walls and floors were wet and the atmosphere inside was "deadly." . . .

Sacco told how he was looked over in the Brockton Police Station by Miss Splaine, Miss Devlin and a good many more identifying witnesses; how he was made to crouch and pretend to aim a pistol; how a cap was put on his head and then his hair was ruffled up. Some of the people shook their heads, he said, and one witness said, "No, sir!"

8

Closing Remarks

The storm had broken the heat, but only temporarily. Shortly after the last crack of thunder, the humidity again descended on Dedham, covering the town in a thick blanket of muggy air and cloaking Judge Thayer's courtroom in a solemn silence.

Today, July 13, was the day for closing arguments, the last chance for the lawyers to summarize their evidence. Each attorney was given two hours to speak.

Defense attorney Fred Moore went first. He spent much of his time urging the jury to ignore the fact that the defendants were anarchists.

You must not think of them as foreigners or radicals. You must put out of your minds the political beliefs of these two young men and look only at the evidence that was presented to you.

Moore also attacked the credibility of the prosecution's witnesses. When he was through making a point, he'd make it again. And again. He begged. He pleaded. He slapped the oak railing of the jury box with his open palm, pearls of sweat flying off his forehead.

There is no justice here, he said. *Look at the testimony; there is absolutely nothing to it. Not one iota of evidence puts these men in South Braintree, let alone on Pearl Street, in the getaway car, or holding a gun!*

After two hours and an extra twenty minutes, Moore sat down, his voice raw, his starched collar drenched, his emotions drained.

Moore's co-counsel, Jeremiah McAnarney, went next. He spoke to the jury and addressed the many holes in the prosecution's case. The twelve men fidgeted in their seats, their jackets off, their sleeves rolled up.

You wouldn't kill a dog based on this evidence, McAnarney said. *Not one of their witnesses was reliable. The only evidence the prosecution has against the defendants is that they happened to be alive when the crime took place.*

Finally, it was Katzmann's turn. The district attorney stood up and walked toward the jury box. As a seasoned lawyer, he surely knew he had little evidence against Nicola, and even less against Bartolomeo. The gatekeeper who had identified Bartolomeo in the getaway car—Michael Levangie—had been discredited by three other witnesses. Still, Katzmann told the jury not to throw away his testimony.

Perhaps Levangie got part of the story wrong, Katzmann said. *But if you think he honestly meant to tell the truth, there's no reason to reject what he said.*

He then moved on to a critical part of his summation: the lies that Nicola and Bartolomeo had told during their arrest.

The defendants said they lied because they thought they were being arrested for their political views. Rubbish! What were they afraid of? Deportation? Gentlemen, they ask you to swallow that! Well, that's simply an absurd defense.

Katzmann took the jurors back over the crime, insisting that the prosecution witnesses were reliable and that the bullet that killed Berardelli did, in fact, come from Nicola's gun.

You heard from the witnesses I brought in here, he said. *Mary Splaine? Do you really think she would condemn a man to death by willfully lying?*

He also defended Lola Andrews, the woman who fainted on the stand, the woman whose testimony was contradicted by two other witnesses.

I have been in this office, gentlemen, for more than eleven years, he said. *I've never laid eye or given ear to a witness as convincing as Lola Andrews.*

Katzmann continued for four hours, twice his allotted time. At seven o'clock in the evening, he finally wrapped up his argument with one more tug on the jurors' patriotic heartstrings, one more thinly veiled reminder that as Americans, they shouldn't excuse the actions of those two anarchists.

"Stand together, you men of Norfolk!" he said.

If he'd been given any more latitude from Judge Thayer, he might have begun singing *Glory, glory, hallelujah* from "The Battle Hymn of the Republic."

After more than eight hours of summations, the jurors, exhausted, sweaty, and dazed, were led out of the courtroom. The fate of the two defendants now rested in their hands.

■ ■ ■

The Verdict

Finally, it was judgment day.

On July 14, after thirty-seven days of eyewitness testimony, ballistics evidence, cross-examinations, and closing arguments, the jurors were set to decide if Nicola and Bartolomeo would live or die.

The trial of Bartolomeo Vanzetti (left) and Nicola Sacco came to a close on July 14, 1921.

True to the morning ritual, eight officers had pulled the two defendants from their jail cells, handcuffed them, marched them through the courtroom, and locked them inside the iron cage.

The courtroom was jam-packed. Spectators crammed into the long oak benches, shoulder to shoulder, their armpits, necks, and brows glistening with sweat. Rosina, desperate to hear good news, brought Dante and sat next to the cage with an anxious, hopeful look on her face.

Judge Thayer looked down at the crowd, the fan on his desk humming away. He ordered the jurors out of the room and called Moore and Katzmann to the bench for a conference. As the three men huddled together, Rosina and Dante scooted over to the prisoners, and Nicola and Bartolomeo playfully tousled Dante's hair. *Boston Globe* reporter Frank P. Sibley caught sight of the moment: "Bartolomeo's eyes glowed, his smile wrinkled his face and crows' feet round his eyes, and the little party seemed very merry."

When the jurors filed back into the room, Rosina and Dante returned to their seats, and Thayer addressed the twelve men: *Summon up your courage, gentlemen. And remember that all classes of society, regardless of their education, money, and resources, have the same rights under the law. Whether these men are rich or poor, radical or conservative, foreign or native-born, they deserve all the privileges that the logic of law, reason, sound judgment, justice, and common sense demand.*

Thayer added there was no doubt that somebody committed murder in the first degree. The question was, who? He then explained the law. "Identity may be established by direct or by circumstantial evidence." In other words, the jury could decide whether Nicola and Bartolomeo were guilty based on the eyewitness statements, however weak those statements may be. As for circumstantial evidence—that is, evidence that is not the result of direct observation—he focused on the issue of "consciousness of guilt."

The questions you need to ask yourselves involve the night the defendants were arrested. Why did they leave the Johnson house? Was it because the car had an outdated license plate or because they'd gotten scared when Mrs. Johnson went to her neighbor's house? And why did they lie to the police? What were they hiding? Murder? If so, that's consciousness of guilt.

At roughly three o'clock in the afternoon, Thayer sent the jurors out of the courtroom to deliberate—taking one last opportunity to stoke their patriotism. *Foreman and gentlemen of the jury*, he said, *even though you knew that jury service would be arduous, painful, and tiresome, you, like the true soldier, responded to that call in the spirit of supreme American loyalty.*

At long last, the jury began to decide the fate of the defendants. Throughout history, lawyers, judges, and defendants refer to these hours—when the jury is sequestered and everyone else is hanging on the decision—as the most anxious of all.

The clock was now ticking on the verdict—and on Nicola and Bartolomeo. The prosecutors and the defense attorneys were adversaries, but they generally agreed on one thing: the longer the jury deliberated, the better the odds were for the defendants. After all, getting twelve patriotic Americans to agree that two anarchists could walk freely out the door was not going to happen in minutes.

The jury worked until just after six o'clock, then broke for supper. At 7:30, Judge Thayer, the prosecutors, and the defense lawyers, tired of waiting in the hot, cramped hallways of the courthouse, walked outside into the cooler evening air. As they lingered on the steps of the courthouse, small crowds began to fill the surrounding streets. With dusk settling in, the only light came from the second-story window where the jurors were holed up.

At 7:55, a knock came from inside the jurors' room. The verdict had been reached.

The sheriff telephoned the jail and ordered the prisoners back to the courthouse. Again Nicola and Bartolomeo were marched through the streets and put back in their cage.

The jurors shuffled into the courtroom, each with his head bowed.

Bartolomeo crunched his forehead. His eyes filled with terror, and his long, droopy mustache failed to conceal a quivering top lip. Next to him, Nicola glanced at the jurors and a sickly expression washed over his face.

Judge Thayer instructed the court clerk to take the verdict from the foreman, Walter Ripley. The jurors stood in their box, as did Nicola and Bartolomeo in their cage.

"Nicola Sacco," the clerk said. "Hold up your right hand."

Nicola did as he was told, his dark eyes begging for mercy.

The clerk turned to Ripley. "What say you, Mr. Foreman. Is the prisoner at the bar guilty or not guilty?"

Ripley bowed his head slightly. "Guilty," he said, his voice trembling.

"Guilty of murder?"

"Yes, murder."

"Murder in the first degree?"

"Yes."

"Upon each indictment?"

"Yes, sir."

After a short, silent pause, the clerk ordered Bartolomeo to raise his right hand. The same questions were again directed at Ripley.

"Mr. Foreman, look upon the prisoner. What say you, is Bartolomeo guilty or not guilty of murder?"

"Guilty."

"In the first degree, upon each indictment?"

"In the first degree."

The clerk then turned to the jury. "You, gentlemen, say that Nicola Sacco and Bartolomeo Vanzetti is each guilty of murder in the first degree upon each indictment. So say you, Mr. Foreman. So, gentlemen, you all say."

The jury responded, "We do, we do, we do."

The courtroom went silent. Bartolomeo appeared stunned; he stared straight ahead, his hand still hanging limply in the air, the color of his olive skin now a pasty white.

Rosina shattered the silence. Bursting into tears, she ran to Nicola, threw her arms around him, and buried her face in his neck—leaving those in the room to stare at nothing but a bun of red hair and two bobbing shoulders. The lawyers tried to pry her off her husband, but she wouldn't let go. Nicola, who'd said little throughout the trial, told them not to touch her. Then he drew her even closer.

"What am I going to do?" she screamed. "I've got two children. O Nick! They kill my man!"

Nicola, shaking, held her to his chest and whispered into her ear.

As Thayer left the bench, Nicola raised his arms into the air.

"Don't forget!" he yelled at the judge. "Two innocent men they kill!"

Finally, a courtroom officer pulled Rosina away. Twenty-five police officers surrounded the condemned prisoners and marched them back to their cells. The crowd outside, having heard the news, surged toward Nicola and Bartolomeo, shouting words of support and outrage as the deputy sheriff ordered them back.

In the courtroom, Assistant District Attorney Harold Williams gathered his papers. A colleague walked over to him, stuck out his hand, and congratulated him. It was, in the eyes of the prosecution, a brilliant victory. Williams looked up, his eyes red-rimmed and watery. "For God's sake, don't rub it in," he said. "This is the saddest thing that ever happened to me in my life."

Shortly after the verdict was read, Judge Thayer reportedly told a friend, "Did you see what I did to those anarchist bastards the other day?"

The Boston Post *announces the verdict.*

Bartolomeo to Elizabeth Glendower Evans (translated from Italian), from Charlestown State Prison

July 22, 1921

My Dear Mrs. Glendower Evans,

Thank you from the bottom of my heart for your faith in my innocence; I am innocent. I have not spilled a drop of blood, nor stolen a penny in all my life.

I don't care about money. My father owns fields, a house, and a garden. He deals in wine and fruits and grain. He has written to me many times to come home and go into his business. Well, this supposed murderer said that his conscience wouldn't permit him to be a businessman. I don't want to earn my bread from that kind of work. I am a child of nature; I'm so rich I don't need money.

Your assistance and the assistance of so many good men and women have made my cross much lighter. I won't forget it.

Please forgive this long letter, but I feel so close to you that a hundred pages wouldn't be enough to express my feelings.

Yours,
Bartolomeo

PART THREE

POSTTRIAL

1921–1927

9

"Save Sacco and Vanzetti"

A handful of journalists pecked at their typewriters in a cramped second-floor office on Hanover Street in Boston's Italian North End. This was the Sacco-Vanzetti Defense Committee, the same group that had raised money to hire Fred Moore to take on Nicola and Bartolomeo's defense after their arrest.

Perhaps no other supporters were more aware of the case than this cohort. They'd seen the huge black letters screaming from the top half of the *Boston Post*'s front page: "GUILTY OF MURDER IN 1ST DEGREE." But they also knew that outside of New England, newspapers had stopped sending reporters to cover the trial. By the time the verdict had been announced, most papers had dropped the names Sacco and Vanzetti from their headlines, banishing them to the inside pages or not mentioning them at all.

A tall Italian fellow wearing wire-framed spectacles was stacking bundles of newspapers by the staircase.

These all need to go out today! he shouted, his baritone voice projecting over the incessant clack of typewriter keys.

The voice belonged to Aldino Felicani, the thirty-year-old head of the committee. With his friend Bartolomeo facing death, Felicani was committed to a single mission: tell the world that Nicola and Bartolomeo had been wrongly convicted based on their status as foreigners, labor supporters, and committed anarchists. Along with two of his colleagues, journalist Eugene Lyons and committee secretary Frank Lopez, he published a newsletter

Aldino Felicani, the head of the Sacco-Vanzetti Defense Committee

called *L'Agitazione* (Agitation) and distributed it in Italy, Spain, and Mexico. From Italy, the paper would go to France. From those four countries, it could wind up almost anywhere.

Felicani tossed another bundle on the heap and directed a half-dozen teenage volunteers waiting by the staircase. *Get these on the truck, now!*

Within months, Felicani's efforts began to pay off. From that dingy office, with virtually no resources of which to speak, the committee triggered a reaction that was impossible to ignore.

The loudest cries of sympathy came from Europe's leftist radicals. They didn't see in Nicola and Bartolomeo a pair of murderers; they saw two young men who had chased the American dream, venturing off to a new country with no skills, no money, and almost no grasp of the English language. In return, they'd been treated as if they were the enemy. In a country that prided itself on free expression, they couldn't speak their minds. When they tried, they'd been rounded up in police raids, arrested, and caged for no good reason.

The campaign hit every corner of the globe—and, in so doing, resurrected the story in American newspapers.

RADICALS OF THE WORLD RESPOND TO CRY SENT FROM BOSTON TO 'SAVE SACCO AND VANZETTI'
Pittsburgh Post

APPEAL OF RADICALS SENT AROUND THE WORLD
Philadelphia Inquirer

A NEW ENGLAND MURDER IS AGITATING FIFTEEN NATIONS
San Francisco Chronicle

Ink alone wasn't enough to satisfy Felicani. "I had to do something," he said. "Friendship for me is something sacred. That is my religion—friendship."

Felicani and fellow supporters organized demonstrations, speeches, labor rallies, and press conferences, gaining the support of scholars, journalists, laborers, and prominent citizens. Volunteers sold pamphlets; solicited donations from the American Fund for Public Service and the Workers' Defense Union; and passed hats at mass meetings for dimes, nickels, even pennies. All the money went

The Sacco-Vanzetti Defense Committee welcomed contributions of any size.

toward the cost of appealing the verdict and, hopefully, getting a new trial for Nicola and Bartolomeo.

Through it all, the committee continued to fire off letters, pamphlets, and journals. There were even buttons made up with the plea "HELP SACCO & VANZETTI."

All these efforts presented a common theme: Any foreigner could be ground up by the American justice system.

■ ■ ■

Protests, Bombs, Grenades

The committee's words spread from continent to continent.

As one newspaper put it, "Switzerland heard the cry from Paris: Paris from Italy: Italy from the little office in Boston . . . Brussels heard of it through the Communist organization across the continent . . . It reached Algiers . . . And from Africa, one may trace the movement to Mexico, to South America, to Porto Rico . . . Brazil answered, Havana answered . . . Lisbon answered."

Suddenly, protesters were demonstrating in all corners of the world, demanding justice for Nicola and Bartolomeo.

A bomb went off in Paris's Salle Wagram, a famous concert hall and meeting space. A hand grenade exploded at the home of the U.S. ambassador to France. Another bomb was intercepted at the American consulate in Lisbon. The police arrested more than a hundred protesters in Rome.

Sympathizers demonstrate in France.

Anatole France, the winner of the 1921 Nobel Prize in Literature, expressed his outrage over the fate of Nicola and Bartolomeo. Writing in the *Nation* magazine, he posted an appeal to the American people: "Sacco and Vanzetti have been condemned for a crime of opinion. It is horrible to think that human beings should pay with their lives for the exercise of that most sacred right . . . Do not let this most iniquitous of sentences be carried out. The death of

Sacco and Vanzetti would make martyrs of them, and would cover all of you with shame. You are a great people; you ought to be a just people."

France, along with two other French writers, Henri Barbusse and Romain Rolland, sent a cablegram to Warren Harding in the White House: "We implore the President of the United States to realize that innumerable hearts throughout the world await with anguish the pardon of Sacco and Vanzetti and hope passionately that great America will do this, which all humanity would applaud."

They received no reply.

Nicola to friends (translated from Italian), from the Dedham jail

November 1921

My Dearest Comrades,

I don't know how to thank the many noble and generous hearts that have embraced the cause of two humble workers. The echo of shouts of thousands and thousands of proletarians reaches my ears and revives me with a Herculean courage . . . The efforts and sacrifices of my comrades are a hymn of victory and justice!

Nicola

Bartolomeo to his sister Luigia (translated from Italian), from Charlestown State Prison

December 1921
Dearest Sister,
   If Christmas means peace of mind and of heart, for me every day is Christmas. I find myself weakened in neither body nor spirit. Our cause is going well . . . I comfort you with the hope of a satisfactory resolution that will return me to those I love and set me free.
   Courage, courage, courage.
                                    Your brother Bartolomeo

10

"I Kept Them Alive"

In the American justice system, a verdict often marks the end of a legal battle. For Nicola and Bartolomeo, it was just the beginning. The next move was to appeal the verdict, and there was no time to waste. They could both be executed in a matter of months.

Only four days after the jury announced its decision, defense attorney Fred Moore formally requested a new trial. That is, he filed a motion—and he kept at it, filing another and another. He flooded the system with so much paperwork that the court had no choice but to delay Nicola's and Bartolomeo's executions until it had a chance to respond to all of Moore's motions.

His actions were not without merit. He challenged Judge Thayer's conduct during the trial, along with jury foreman Walter Ripley's stated bias against the defendants. He also presented a list of witnesses who, after the trial, had retracted their testimony.

Ballistics expert and police captain William H. Proctor claimed that Katzmann had twisted his words. He'd never concluded that Sacco's gun had fired the bullet that killed Berardelli.

Louis Pelser, the man who'd identified Sacco as the gunman,

signed an affidavit admitting he'd lied under oath. He said the prosecuting attorney Harold Williams had pressured him into fingering Nicola. "I don't think I was exactly sane," he wrote. "They certainly had me on my head. I didn't realize what I was answering to."

Lola Andrews, the woman who fainted on the stand, said that her identification of Nicola had been "unqualifiedly false and untrue" and had been made "under the intimidating and coercing influence" of Katzmann's office. In the words of the *Boston American*, "She is either crazy or someone in the district attorney's office at that time ought to be arrested for attempted murder."

Moore also presented statements from new witnesses. One came from Roy Gould, a traveling salesman who had been walking on Railroad Avenue in South Braintree on April 15, 1920, the day of the crime. Gould had seen the robbery and had come within five feet of the getaway car; he was so close that one of the killers' bullets tore through his overcoat. During the buildup to the trial, he'd been shown a photo of Nicola by the district attorney—and insisted Nicola wasn't the gunman. But his words were ignored, and he was never put on the stand. Moore felt that Gould's testimony, a critical piece of evidence, had been buried by the prosecution.

But the Massachusetts legal system prevented Moore's arguments from landing in front of fresh eyes. The law said that all posttrial motions were to be decided by the same judge who had presided at the trial. In other words, the only person who could overrule Judge Thayer on these motions was Judge Thayer.

To nobody's surprise, Thayer denied them all.

Moore spent three years trying to secure a new trial, but in 1924, he gave up and submitted his resignation to the court. With no reason to stay in Massachusetts, he got into his beat-up car and left town, still at odds with the court—and with the Sacco-Vanzetti Defense Committee. Felicani and his cohorts felt that Moore could have done a better job defending Nicola and Bartolomeo, that he'd allowed the case to get away from him, that he'd allowed Thayer to control the direction of the trial.

Moore had been defeated time and again, but he drove back to the West Coast with his head held high.

"At least I kept them alive," he said.

To save Nicola and Bartolomeo from the electric chair, the committee sprang into action, persuading William Thompson to take over the case. Given Thompson's reputation as one of Boston's most respected lawyers, the committee figured he'd be able to navigate the land mines seeded throughout the Massachusetts legal system.

But even Thompson, joining the fray years after the trial, failed to bring much in the way of results.

Unless Thompson found some new piece of evidence that would clear his clients, Nicola and Bartolomeo would never be saved from the grinding wheels of the American justice system.

■ ■ ■

Behind Bars

Nicola spent twenty-three hours a day in a fifty-square-foot cell that barely fit a table and his sliver of a bed; his only physical activity was an hour in the Dedham jail yard. At night, when the lights went out, he paced the tiny space, counting his steps, one, two, three, four, five, stopping only to gaze through his barred window at a slice of exposed sky. During the day, to spell the boredom, he sat at the small wooden table and wrote letters to his supporters. In so many of those messages, he spoke of his children, how his daughter, Ines, visited him, how she would leap into his arms with hugs and kisses. Judging by his letters, if Nicola had his way, Rosina, Dante, and Ines would leap off his inked pages. They'd come to life right there in his cell, the four of them living as a family while he waited for his defense team to come back with news of a retrial.

Bartolomeo filled his days at the Charlestown State Prison working in the print shop or the library. Back in his cell, he wrote dozens of essays and articles that appeared in radical newspapers. He also penned a memoir, *The Story of a Proletarian Life*, which featured an appreciation by the well-known socialist writer Upton Sinclair. Ever a man of letters, Bartolomeo also took a correspondence course to improve his English language skills. But without a wife or child to provide moral support, or perhaps because he was confined in a decrepit prison, he couldn't handle the pressure of being incarcerated. In 1924, his nervous system snapped under the stress, spiraling him into a pit of despair and delirium. He was removed to a psychiatric hospital, where he spent four months convalescing but never fully recovered.

While at the hospital, he received a letter from Nicola.

"My Dear Comrade Vanzetti," Nicola wrote. "This morning . . . my first thought was to write you these few lines, and send you my most kind and warm wish for your birthday, with hope that it will be the last of yours and mine birthdays that we spend in [prison] . . . Well, my dear comrade, we must always hope that someday the sunshine will brighten our souls again."

Nicola's message brought little cheer.

Bartolomeo was buckling, physically and mentally. The only thing that could save him was freedom, but so far, every dream he'd had of a new trial had been dashed by a stacked, one-sided legal system.

■ ■ ■

"I Hear By Confess"

On November 18, 1925, a glimmer of hope found its way to Nicola by way of a fellow prisoner at Dedham jail.

This is from the Spanish guy down the row, a guard said, slipping a rolled-up magazine through the bars of Nicola's cell.

Nicola took the magazine and found a loose note within its pages. The scrawled letter came from a Portuguese-born inmate who had been sentenced to death for killing a bank clerk in a holdup strikingly similar to the one in South Braintree.

The message was short, chilling, and exhilarating: "I hear by confess to being in the south Braintree shoe company crime and Sacco and Vanzetti was not in said crime." It was signed, "Celestino F. Madeiros."

Nicola read it again and again, making sure he wasn't misunderstanding the words—but there was only one way to interpret their meaning. Madeiros was confessing to the South Braintree murders. Nicola paced in a small circle, his heart racing, his energy bubbling over, his body yearning to run, to jump, to plow through the jail's stone walls.

As soon as he could, he contacted attorney William Thompson, who arranged to meet with Madeiros at the jail. It wasn't long before the twenty-three-year-old inmate was explaining to Thompson that he couldn't hide the truth any longer, that his heart went out to Nicola's wife and children. He said he had tried to confess to Nicola before, but Nicola was suspicious of Madeiros and afraid to talk

Celestino Madeiros, member of the Joe Morelli gang

with a stranger about his case. And so Madeiros had scribbled his message on a piece of paper and sent it along the cellblock via special delivery.

With nothing to gain and everything to lose, Madeiros laid out the details about the South Braintree robbery, signing a confession that answered all the questions surrounding the case.

According to Madeiros, he was on Pearl Street, sitting in the back of the Buick, holding a revolver, when his cohorts gunned down Parmenter and Berardelli. The driver, following the plan, drove up Pearl so the killers could jump in with the money boxes. Then the crew sped out of town.

As Police Chief Michael Stewart had suspected, the bandits used two cars. Starting out in a Hudson, they'd driven to the woods, dumped the car, and piled into the Buick to make their way to South

Braintree. But Stewart had been only half-right: The men had never gone to Puffer's Place, nor were they connected to Mike Boda or, for that matter, Boda's Overland.

Instead, Madeiros fingered the Morelli gang, a bunch of freight train robbers from Providence, Rhode Island. Either out of honor or fear, he wouldn't name his partners, but he did describe them and their ethnicities and said the two men who'd shot Parmenter and Berardelli were Italian. After the killings, he said, the gang had driven back to the woods, scrambled out of the Buick and into the Hudson, and raced back to Providence.

To prove he wasn't lying, he even told Thompson that he'd taken his share of the stolen money, $2,800, and spent it on a trip to Mexico.

Thompson launched into his own investigation to ensure that Madeiros's account of the crime held up. He looked into the Morelli gang and found witnesses who verified this new version of events.

The pieces fell into place like a set of building blocks. Joe Morelli owned a .32-caliber Colt. His brother Mike drove a Buick that disappeared immediately after the crime. The Providence police had even kept an eye on the Morelli gang, suspecting it might be behind the South Braintree murders. But when Nicola and Bartolomeo were arrested, the cops lost interest.

Convinced there were no holes in Madeiros's account, Thompson filed a motion for a new trial. Then he and Nicola and Bartolomeo waited, hanging on the court's decision.

A few months later, they got their answer.

Judge Thayer denied the motion, claiming that Madeiros's confession didn't match the facts that had come out during the trial. He also took issue with Madeiros's inability to describe the crime scene, particularly the water tower, the railroad crossing, and the shoe factories. Thompson pointed out that Madeiros had barely seen Pearl Street; he'd been sitting in the back of the Buick with the curtains drawn when the murders were committed. Plus, it was only natural that Madeiros's memory would be foggy; he'd spent the hours leading up to the crime drinking bootleg spirits to calm his nerves.

But Thayer's mind was made up: Madeiros's confession was unreliable, untrustworthy, and untrue. The man "has been convicted and sentenced to death" for murder, Thayer wrote in his response. "Madeiros is, without doubt, a crook, a thief, a robber, a liar, a rum-runner, a 'bouncer' in a house of ill-fame, a smuggler."

Thompson then appealed the conviction to the state's highest court—which meant that a panel of judges, not Thayer, would review the case. Still, the court sided with Thayer and upheld the conviction.

Nicola and Bartolomeo were doomed.

■ ■ ■

Marking Time

On April 9, 1927, with all appeals exhausted, Nicola and Bartolomeo were sentenced to die in the electric chair.

Their executions were set for the week of July 10.

Prison officials collected the two men from their beds and brought them to the Cherry Hill section of the Charlestown State Prison to wait out their final days. Battered physically and emotionally, they sat in cells adjacent to the execution chamber, marking time as the end drew near.

With renewed urgency, the Sacco-Vanzetti Defense Committee kicked into overdrive. They dashed off letters, issued public appeals, and gathered petitions in a last-minute attempt to sway the court, hoping to prolong the defendants' lives. Aldino Felicani, desperate and determined, also wrote editorials in international newspapers, begging the world for help.

The public responded.

Telegrams flooded the offices of the committee. According to Felicani, "They came from every corner of the earth. We had messages from South Africa, from Russia, from South America, from England, from Germany, from France. We had messages from the most prominent human beings everywhere. They were all the same messages, 'If we can help, let us know.'"

The outcry was too loud, and too constant, to ignore.

Protesters demonstrate in Australia.

Succumbing to public pressure, Massachusetts Governor Alvan T. Fuller delayed the execution thirty days so that he could reexamine the case. For Nicola and Bartolomeo, Fuller was their only hope. He had the authority to provide executive clemency, meaning he could issue a pardon—freeing them of all charges—or at the very least, lift the death penalty and allow them to continue living behind bars.

Fuller appointed a committee, headed by Harvard University President A. Lawrence Lowell, to consider the issue of clemency. From July 11 to July 21, the committee reviewed seven thousand pages of trial testimony and interviewed nearly two hundred witnesses.

While the committee was at work, Fuller visited the prison to speak with the defendants face-to-face.

Nicola, convinced the system was rigged, refused to shake the governor's hand.

Bartolomeo, though, chatted with Fuller for nearly two hours. The next morning he met with his friend Felicani and said, "[Governor Fuller] talked to me like a brother, smiling and joking. That man will never send us to the chair."

But on August 3, the governor did just that. He denied clemency after the Lowell Committee declared that the trial, and the subsequent appeals process, had been fair "on the whole."

Columnist Heywood Broun, referring to Harvard as "Hangman's House," wrote sarcastically of the decision, "What more can these immigrants from Italy expect? It is not every prisoner who has a president of Harvard University throw the switch for him."

On August 10, Governor Fuller delayed the execution another

twelve days, allowing Thompson and his team to appeal to the U.S. Supreme Court. But that court refused to take the case.

Thompson was out of moves. He'd tried every avenue and repeatedly been shut down.

On August 21, 1927, time was running out for Nicola and Bartolomeo.

Taking command of his own fate, Nicola went on a hunger strike, his second since being convicted. He refused food for more than three weeks, but he backed down when prison officials threatened to force-feed him.

Bartolomeo, also desperate to control his own destiny, picked up the sheet covering his bed, ripped it into strips, tied the pieces together, and wound them around his throat. He then attached the loose, dangling end of the sheet to the iron brace above the door, climbed on top of the bureau, and swung himself into the air. Just as he let go, his foot caught the end of the bureau, tipping it over with a crash that alerted the guards—who raced in and saved his life.

Just in time to put him and Nicola to death.

Nicola to his daughter, Ines, from Charlestown State Prison

July 19, 1927

My Dear Ines,

I am going to try from the bottom of my heart to make you understand how dear you are to your father's soul . . . I know that you will save this letter and read it over in future years to come and you will see and feel the same heart-beat affection as your father feels in writing it to you.

I will bring with me your little and so dearest letter and carry it right under my heart to the last day of my life. When I die, it will be buried with your father who loves you so much as I do also your brother Dante and holy dear mother.

You do not know, Ines, how often I think of you every day. You are in my heart, my vision, in every angle of this sad walled cell, in the sky and everywhere my gaze rests.

Your Father

Nicola to his son, Dante, from Charlestown State Prison

August 18, 1927

My Dear Son and Companion,

I never thought that our inseparable life could be separated . . . Son, instead of crying, be strong, so as to be able to comfort your mother . . . take her for a long walk in the quiet country, gathering wild flowers here and there, resting under the shade of trees . . . Remember always, Dante . . . help the weak ones that cry for help, help the prosecuted and the victim . . . they are the comrades that fight and fall as your father and Bartolo fought and fell yesterday for the conquest of the joy of freedom for all.

Your Father and Companion

11

August 23, 1927

Nicola and Bartolomeo were scheduled to die at midnight on Tuesday, August 23, 1927.

Knowing a wave of demonstrators would descend upon the city, the police took measures never before seen in Boston. On Monday evening, August 22, nearly half the force—more than eight hundred officers—surrounded the Charlestown State Prison on horses and motorcycles, armed with guns and nightsticks. Those on foot lined the top of the death house, brandishing machine guns. They patrolled the grounds, toting containers of tear gas. And they

Police guard the death house, August 22, 1927.

manned marine boats stationed in the river nearby, beaming search-lights onto the brick facade of the hulking old prison.

They closed the local streets. They told residents to stay indoors. And they ordered gas stations and shops to shut down until Wednesday.

The crowds came anyway.

On Monday morning, hundreds of sympathizers gathered on Main Street, turning the area into a tangled mess of demonstrators, private cars, and commercial vehicles. Police barked out orders, but they were outmatched by the surging crowd. Protesters marched and shouted. Cars blared their horns. When the marchers approached the barricades, the cops, nightsticks in hand, pushed them back, swinging when it was necessary—and sometimes when it wasn't.

At nearby Thompson Square, the police intercepted a procession making its way from the State House to the prison. Mounted police officers beat back the crowd, rearing their horses high and bringing them down violently.

A little before nine o'clock in the evening, Prison Warden William Hendry met with Nicola and Bartolomeo, as well as Celestino Madeiros, the Portuguese inmate who'd confessed to the South Braintree murders—and who was scheduled to die that same night for the bank-clerk killing.

When Hendry reached Madeiros's cell, he found the condemned man sound asleep in his bunk. Madeiros woke up momentarily and then rolled over and went back to sleep. A few days earlier, though, Madeiros had spoken with Aldino Felicani, who'd come to the prison to support Nicola and Bartolomeo.

"Too bad for them," Madeiros had told Felicani. "Me, I'm a criminal anyhow; I have a long record. But them—it's a shame for them."

When Hendry entered Nicola's cell, Nicola was just finishing a letter to his father. He gave the note to the warden, along with two requests.

Be sure this letter is mailed to my father. And when I'm dead, send my body back to Italy.

At ten o'clock, the chief electrician, Granville Greenough, and his assistant, John Mullaney, entered the prison to test the equipment: the switches on the wall that would send out more than a thousand volts of electricity, the wires that would carry the current to the electric chair, the electrodes that would attach to the prisoner's head and legs, the skullcap that would be strapped to his head, and the leather straps that would hold his body in place when it jerked from the electricity.

The execution chamber at Charlestown State Prison with electric chair on left

When the electricians finished, they assured the warden everything was in working order.

Around eleven o'clock, firemen gathered outside the death house, armed with high-pressure hoses, ready to put out any flames caused by the overloaded high-voltage wires.

One contingent of police lined up on the roof of the State House, a mile away from the prison, riot guns in hand. Another switched on searchlights and swept the beams over the local streets, briefly illuminating the throng that filled the roads in a silent vigil—along with entire families, including mothers clutching infants, perched on rooftops.

At 11:38, inside the prison, officials stood by specially installed telephones and telegraphs, ready to spread news of the executions to the world.

And Nicola and Bartolomeo, having refused any support from the clergy, prepared to take the seventeen-step walk from their cells to the death chamber, alone.

■ ■ ■

"Long Live Anarchy"

At eleven minutes past midnight, Nicola was brought into the death chamber, a small, stark white room. He was barely able to stand; his hunger strike had taken its toll on him. He looked frail and weak in his standard gray prison garb, far older than his thirty-six years. His eyes were deep and dark, his cheeks hollow.

Ten minutes earlier, Celestino Madeiros, at one time Nicola's only hope for freedom, had made the same journey. He had gone to the chair in a daze, shrugged his shoulders, and said nothing as the guards buckled the dangling straps around his arms and torso. The five witnesses, seated a few feet away, watched as his body spasmed and then went still.

The smell of his burnt flesh still lingered in the room.

Nicola could take comfort knowing that Rosina wasn't alone during these agonizing moments, that she was with Bartolomeo's sister Luigia at a nearby apartment, awaiting the outcome. When they had said their goodbyes earlier in the day, Nicola reached through the bars of his cell to grasp Rosina's hands.

"I love you," he said. "And I always will."

"Nick," she said. "I am dying with you."

When she walked away, he took one last glimpse of the woman with the rust-colored hair and soft brown eyes who had won his heart more than fifteen years earlier.

Now he walked to the center of the chamber, his knees wobbling. When he sat down in the chair, the guards rolled up his trouser cuffs, strapped his ankles into the stirrups, and attached electrodes to his shaved skin.

He shouted in Italian, "Viva l'anarchia!" (Long live anarchy!) Then he closed his eyes, and in English said, "Farewell, my wife and child, and all my friends." No doubt Nicola's difficulty with English and the anguish he was feeling caused him to say "child" instead of "children."

The guards slipped a mask over his face and attached the skullcap.

"Farewell, Mother," he said, his voice muffled by the cloth covering his face.

The executioner pulled the switch and hit Nicola with nearly two thousand volts of electricity. Nicola's body had lost so much water and salt during his hunger strike that the executioner needed to add extra current.

His body lurched forward, straining against the leather straps, and the lights in the room dimmed. After ten seconds, the executioner returned the switch to the off position and the lights brightened again.

Nicola was pronounced dead at 12:19 a.m.

Bartolomeo followed a minute later. Unlike Nicola, Bartolomeo, now thirty-nine, still appeared healthy. To keep his sanity, he, too, had written letters until the final moments—one to his sister Luigia, whom he had seen hours earlier when they said their final goodbyes.

He stopped and shook hands with the two guards who led him into the chamber.

As he sat in the death seat, he said, "I wish to tell you that I am innocent and that I never committed any crime but sometimes some sin."

He then uttered his final words: "I wish to forgive some people for what they are now doing to me."

The room fell silent, and then the executioner threw the switch.

Bartolomeo was pronounced dead at 12:26.

Warden Hendry looked on with tears in his eyes. Speaking in a whisper, he said the words required of him: "Under the law I now pronounce you dead, the sentence of the court having been legally carried out."

Thirty minutes later, the bodies of Nicola and Bartolomeo—and that of Celestino Madeiros—were placed inside an ambulance and driven to the mortuary.

Madeiros's body was then taken to the town of New Bedford, where he had lived since arriving in America as a young child. The bodies of Nicola and Bartolomeo were delivered to undertaker Joseph A. Langone in Boston's North End.

Meanwhile, outside the prison, the demonstrators slowly, and silently, dispersed.

In the words of a United Press reporter, "The rambling old prison was left brooding under the moonless sky. Its prisoners, tensely awake but quiet during the executions, returned to sleep."

New York Daily News, *August 23, 1927*

■ ■ ■

The World Protests

On the night of the execution, twenty thousand sympathizers jammed into New York City's Union Square, awaiting word from Boston as to the fates of Nicola and Bartolomeo. When the news arrived, it came in the form of a pair of homemade signs. First, employees at the communist newspaper *Daily Worker* put a sign in their window: SACCO MURDERED. Moments later, they added a second one: VANZETTI MURDERED. The overflowing crowd gasped and moaned and sobbed until their cries faded into utter silence.

Demonstrators in Union Square on the night of the execution

But in Europe, where it was dawn, the reaction was violent and immediate.

In France, protesters detonated a bomb in the Montpellier police station. Mobs raided Paris cafés, throwing chairs and tables through plate-glass windows. Rioters pelted police at the American embassy with canned goods, rocks, and other makeshift weapons, not letting up until the cops rushed at them with military tanks.

In Great Britain, twenty thousand demonstrators clashed with police in London's Hyde Park.

In Germany, a crowd stormed the Leipzig police station, shouting "Revenge!"

In Poland, a mob charged the American consulate in Warsaw.

In the Soviet Union, waves of protesters stormed the streets of Moscow.

In Switzerland, three thousand rioters surrounded the American consulate in Geneva, chanting "Assassins!" and "Down with America!" until police beat them back with high-powered blasts of water from fire hoses. Elsewhere in the city, a movie theater closed "due to mourning." Other businesses refused to serve Americans. Angry mobs stormed American targets, such as Model T cars, shops selling Lucky Strike cigarettes, or movie theaters showing Mary Pickford or Douglas Fairbanks films.

In the eyes of the world, America, which had once been seen as the land of opportunity, was now a place of oppression, injustice, and murder.

■ ■ ■

The March

On Sunday, August 28, a steady rain washed over Boston as mourners inched their way through the undertaker's room, paying their respects to the two fallen anarchists.

Nicola and Bartolomeo lay in rest, their emaciated bodies and pale gray faces lit only by soft candlelight. Elizabeth Glendower Evans, a prominent socialite and steadfast supporter, wrote about the funeral in *La Follette's Magazine*:

> They laid their bodies in a little undertaker's place in the North End of Boston where the Italians live in great number. For three days and late into the night an endless file passed between the coffins and the wall, the space so narrow that time was allowed for scarce more than a glance. There were mounds of flowers upon the coffins and in the corners of the room, and masses of them outside in an entrance room.

Pallbearers carry the caskets containing the bodies of Nicola and Bartolomeo.

In midafternoon, the pallbearers slid the two caskets into a pair of hearses for the drive to Forest Hills Cemetery. A crush of mourners packed the six-mile route, holding signs that read "Martyrs of

Massachusetts" and tossing flowers at the procession, blanketing the path to the cemetery in red blossoms.

If success is measured by the love one engenders in life, Nicola and Bartolomeo died rich men.

Two hundred sympathizers led the march, slowly and respectfully, hoisting up floral arrangements that overflowed with gifts and trinkets from nearly every country in the world. Next came marchers with blood-red bands around their arms and matching carnations in their buttonholes, their fists holding umbrellas but their elbows firmly interlocked.

Theirs was a united front.

Luigia Vanzetti, Rosina Sacco, and fourteen-year-old Dante Sacco came next, seated in the back of a family car with the curtains drawn. Absent was six-year-old Ines Sacco, who was in the care of family friends. Aldino Felicani and fellow members of the Sacco-Vanzetti Defense Committee trailed behind in a separate vehicle, while other mourners filled the procession of cars that followed.

The funeral procession fills Tremont Street in Boston.

The *Boston Globe* reported the scene: "As the procession proceeded along Hanover Street, every one of the hundreds of windows was clustered with heads. The sidewalks were packed solid with people, mostly of Italian origin, who took off their hats or bowed their heads as the hearses passed."

The motorcade inched along, mile after mile, until it arrived at the cemetery, where seventy mounted police and five hundred officers stood guard. Then, the pallbearers carried the bodies into the chapel.

Mary Donovan of the Defense Committee delivered a brief eulogy. With Luigia and Rosina standing close by, Donovan decried the executions as "one of the blackest crimes in the history of mankind."

The caskets were then brought to the crematorium, and in less than an hour, the bodies of Nicola and Bartolomeo were reduced to ash. Their remains would be divided into four copper urns—two for Nicola and two for Bartolomeo.

One urn containing Nicola's ashes would be shipped to his hometown of Torremaggiore; one containing Bartolomeo's would be sent to his birthplace of Villafalletto.

The other two were to be stored in America, but no cemetery around Boston would accept them. Decades later, they found a home inside a vault at the Boston Public Library—alongside the Congressional Gold Medal awarded to George Washington, a lock of hair belonging to John Hancock, and a fifteenth-century copy of a letter written by Christopher Columbus upon his arrival in the New World.

Nicola and Bartolomeo are now as much a part of American history as the country's early founders. They were betrayed by a nation that had offered so much promise, but they remain heroes to the downtrodden and the strivers who still chase their own dreams to America.

Nicola and Bartolomeo to the Sacco-Vanzetti Defense Committee, from the death house of Charlestown State Prison

August 21, 1927
Dear Friends and Comrades,

We decided to write this letter to you to express our gratitude and admiration for all what you have done in our defense during these seven years, four months, and eleven days of struggle.

That we lost and have to die does not diminish our appreciation and gratitude for your great solidarity with us and our families . . .

We embrace you all, and bid you all our extreme good-bye with our hearts filled with love and affection. Now and ever, long life to you all, long life to Liberty.

Yours in life and death,
Bartolomeo Vanzetti
Nicola Sacco

EPILOGUE

For years, the memories of Nicola Sacco and Bartolomeo Vanzetti haunted those around them.

Bartolomeo's sister Luigia never stopped grieving. According to her younger sister, Vincenzina, "She suffered and cried so much that something went out in her brain."

Nicola's wife, Rosina, spent years living in poverty. Eventually she remarried, but she never stopped mourning the loss of Nicola. Long after his execution, she told her daughter-in-law not to bother praying. "I tried it once," she said. "It didn't work."

Nicola's son, Dante, raised three sons of his own, never passing on the story of their grandfather, presumably to free them of the shame associated with the family name.

Nobody involved walked away unscathed.

Five years after the execution, a bomb destroyed Judge Thayer's home. No lives were lost. No bomber was found.

Radical groups also targeted the prosecutor Frederick Katzmann. A special police detail guarded his house for ten years after the jury delivered its verdict.

Fred Moore continued to practice law in the West, still bitter at the Defense Committee for removing him from the case.

The cast of characters is long gone, but Nicola and Bartolomeo live on in popular culture, inspiring songs, movies, books, and plays. Most significant, their case has sparked countless debates over immigration, the death penalty, and the American justice system.

Harvard Law School professor Felix Frankfurter, who also went on to become a U.S. Supreme Court justice, questioned the evidence against Nicola and Bartolomeo, as well as Judge Thayer's conduct during the trial: "In view of the temper of the times, the nature of the accusation, the opinions of the accused, the tactics of the prosecution, and the conduct of the judge, no wonder the 'men of Norfolk' convicted Sacco and Vanzetti!"

Another Supreme Court justice, William O. Douglas, wrote that it was hard to believe the trial had taken place in the United States. If the case had come along in the 1960s, he said, the Supreme Court would have reexamined it for a number of reasons: Thayer's hyper-patriotic language, the way in which the jury was chosen, Proctor's clarification, and the "saturation of the trial with the radicalism of the defendants."

In 1947, on the twentieth anniversary of the executions, Nobel physicist Albert Einstein wrote, "Everything should be done to keep alive the tragic affair of Sacco and Vanzetti in the conscience of mankind. They remind us of the fact that even the most perfectly planned democratic institutions are no better than the people whose instruments they are."

That same year, Einstein and former first lady Eleanor Roosevelt were among the many dignitaries who signed a public declaration requesting that the city of Boston or the state of Massachusetts honor Nicola and Bartolomeo with a sculpture—one that had been created by Gutzon Borglum, the artist who carved Mount Rushmore. The sculpture, however, had already been rejected, repeatedly, by various officials, and was rejected again.

Finally, on August 23, 1977, Massachusetts Governor Michael Dukakis, the son of Greek immigrants, issued a proclamation. Nicola and Bartolomeo had not received a fair trial, he said, and any stigma and disgrace attached to them should be forever removed. In the proclamation, issued in both English and Italian, Dukakis declared that the trial "was permeated by prejudice against foreigners and hostility toward unorthodox political views."

In 1997, Boston Mayor Tom Menino and Massachusetts Governor Paul Cellucci finally accepted Borglum's artwork. It is displayed on the third floor of the Boston Public Library.

Gutzon Borglum's bronze cast preserves the memory of Nicola and Bartolomeo.

Bartolomeo's words on Gutzon Borglum's plaque at the Boston Public Library

"What I wish more than all in this last hour of agony is that our case and our fate may be understood in their real being and serve as a tremendous lesson to the forces of freedom so that our suffering and death will not have been in vain."

ACKNOWLEDGMENTS

When we suggested writing a book about Sacco and Vanzetti, both our original editor, Katherine Jacobs, and our agent, Jennifer Weltz, jumped at the idea. When the time came, Emily Feinberg took the editing reins with equal enthusiasm. Thank you, Jennifer, Katherine, and Emily, for believing in the story.

In taking on this project, we set out to be true to history. And so we acknowledge the journalists who covered the Sacco-Vanzetti trial. They left behind detailed accounts of the proceedings, as well as an insider's look at twentieth-century America, warts and all. When we had to fill a hole in history, we relied on the many authors who've reexamined the case over the past hundred years. When we needed help in deciphering a legal issue, we turned to Amanda Shapiro, Esq. And when we needed a pair of fresh eyes (and a sharper red pen), we entrusted the manuscript with educators Sharman Yoffie-Sidman and Alan Sidman.

We are in their debt.

Somewhere along the line, we realized that the journeys of our own grandparents closely paralleled those of our subjects. With that in mind we thank Nicola, Bartolomeo, and all the immigrants who came to America with empty pockets, full hearts, and a belief that they had found the promised land.

This is their story.

SOURCE NOTES

Throughout the book, whenever possible, we leaned on the writings of Nicola and Bartolomeo to re-create their story, particularly Nicola and Bartolomeo's *Letters of Sacco and Vanzetti* and Bartolomeo's *Il Caso Sacco e Vanzetti*.

We also relied heavily on the trial transcripts, historical newspaper accounts, and three case histories of the Sacco-Vanzetti trial: Paul Avrich's *Sacco and Vanzetti: The Anarchist Background*; Susan Tejada's *In Search of Sacco and Vanzetti: Double Lives, Troubled Times, and the Massachusetts Murder Case That Shook the World*; and Bruce Watson's *Sacco and Vanzetti: The Men, the Murders, and the Judgment of Mankind*.

The following notes address the material we used in addition to these sources.

April 15, 1920

The information regarding the shoe industry is from Mostov's "Immigrant Entrepreneurs" and historical newspapers.

To re-create the crime in South Braintree, we relied heavily on the *Boston Post,* "Bandits Kill Guard and Steal $20,000," and the *Boston Globe*, "Bandits Kill Guard, Shoot Paymaster." We also leaned on the Tejada and Watson case histories and Musmanno's *After Twelve Years*.

The scene in which Frederick Parmenter and Alessandro Berardelli leave the Hampton House was taken from the Tejada case history.

We extrapolated the conversation between Parmenter and Jimmy Bostock from information in the Watson case history.

Chapter 1

The year of Nicola's arrival in the United States is in dispute. Nicola gave the year 1908 during the trial, and most authoritative sources cite the same year. The confusion regards the "alien list" of the S. S. *Romanic*, which indicates he arrived in 1909 under his given name Ferdinando. We have chosen to use the year 1908 to remain true to the Avrich, Tejada, and Watson case histories.

Nicola's arrival on the *Romanic* and his childhood in Torremaggiore are taken from the Avrich and Watson case histories and *Letters of Sacco and Vanzetti*.

To describe America in the early twentieth century, we leaned on Rasenberger's *America, 1908*, along with the Library of Congress's "Work in the Late 19th Century" and "Progressive Era to New Era." The statistic regarding 10 percent of Americans owning nearly all of the country's wealth is from Wagner's *America and the Great War*.

Nicola's experience in the United States is from the Tejada and Watson case histories. We also used those books when creating the conversation between Nicola and Rosina.

For Bartolomeo's story—including his upbringing in Villafalletto, his arrival in the United States, and his experience at Ellis Island—we relied on his *Story of a Proletarian Life*, as well as the Avrich, Tejada, and Watson case histories. We found additional material on Bartolomeo's life with the Brinis in Musmanno's *After Twelve Years* and Avrich's *Anarchist Voices*.

Bartolomeo's quotes about America ("New York loomed on the horizon . . ." and "I seemed to have awakened in a land . . .") are from his *Story of a Proletarian Life*. His quote about New York being "the immense hell pit of the poor" is from *Il Caso Sacco e Vanzetti: Lettere ai familiari* (Editori Riuniti, 1971); we found the translation in the Watson case history.

The quote about Bartolomeo's being "a familiar figure on the streets and byways of Plymouth" is from Musmanno's *After Twelve Years*.

The words of seventy-nine-year-old Beltrando Brini are from Avrich's *Anarchist Voices*.

Chapter 2

Congressmen questioning whether "the south Italian" was "a full-blooded Caucasian" is from the U.S. House of Representatives' *Hearings Relative to the Further Restriction of Immigration*; we found it in Thomas Guglielmo's "Rethinking Whiteness."

We compiled our information on Luigi Galleani from Neville's *Twentieth-Century Cause Célèbre* and the Avrich case history.

The part about dangers in the workplace is from MacLaury's "Progressive Era Investigations" on the U.S. Department of Labor website. The story of the twelve-year-old girl losing her scalp is from the *Boston Globe*, "Warm Hearing." The information regarding the Triangle shirtwaist factory is from McLaughlin's "Was Tragedy of Triangle Girls All in Vain?"

Nicola's words about workers' struggles ("The nightmare of the lower classes . . .") are from *Letters of Sacco and Vanzetti*.

Bartolomeo's idea about anarchism ("a belief in human freedom . . .") is from Flynn's *Rebel Girl*; we found the quote in the Tejada case history.

The section on Nicola and Bartolomeo following Galleani and participating in anarchist activities is taken from the Avrich, Tejada, and Watson case histories. We also relied on D'Attilio's "La Salute è in Voi." Galleani's words ("the soldier who prostitutes himself . . .") come from the May 26, 1917, edition of *Cronaca Sovversiva*; we found the translation in the Watson case history.

The passage on Nicola and Bartolomeo's experience in Mexico is from the Avrich, Tejada, and Watson case histories and *Letters of Sacco and Vanzetti*.

The letter from Bartolomeo to his family is from his *Il Caso Sacco e Vanzetti* (translated by Ouisie Shapiro).

Chapter 3

We found the information regarding the bombings of Senator Hardwick's and Attorney General Palmer's homes in the Avrich and Watson case histories. We also dug into historical newspaper accounts, most notably the *Evening Star* (Washington, D.C.), "Bomb Explosion." Palmer's words are from the United Press, "Sleuths Look to Paterson."

The quote from President Wilson's annual message to Congress ("poured the poison . . . ") can be found at Gerhard Peters and John T. Woolley's American Presidency Project, presidency.ucsb.edu/node/207590.

The information about Senators Overman, Walsh, and King is from the *New York Times*, "Bills to Punish Reds."

Palmer calling the bombings "nothing but a lawless attempt of an anarchistic element" is from his statement in the *Washington Post*, "Attempt to Terrorize Has Failed."

We compiled the material on the Palmer Raids from the newspapers of the day and the Tejada and Watson case histories; other key sources were Hochschild's "When America Tried"; Damon's "Great Red Scare"; the FBI's "A Byte Out of History," on its archived website; and the *Congressional Record*, volume 86, part 19, Senate 7261–73 (May 31, 1940), found at www.govinfo.gov. Palmer's article in the February 1920 issue of *Forum* was titled "The Case Against the 'Reds.'" The quote from the federal agent ("This is your warrant") is from the trial transcript of Colyer v. Skeffington, found at cite.case .law/f/265/17/.

The William O. Douglas quote about the government's actions being disgraceful is from his *Almanac of Liberty*.

Nicola's life in Stoughton, including his escapades with Dante, are from the Avrich case history, Musmanno's *After Twelve Years*, and Neville's *Twentieth-Century Cause Célèbre*.

The information on the strikes from 1919 is from the Tejada and Watson case histories, Murray's *Red Scare*, and Neville's *Twentieth-Century Cause Célèbre*.

We found the stories regarding Andrea Salsedo in *Letters of Sacco and Vanzetti*, Speer's "Nobody Held Liable," and the Avrich, Tejada, and Watson case histories.

Chapter 4

We re-created the scenes with Bridgewater Police Chief Michael Stewart using information from the Watson case history, Joughin and Morgan's *Legacy of Sacco and Vanzetti*, and several newspapers of the day. To create Stewart's conversations with Boda and Johnson, we used the same sources, along with D'Attilio's "La Salute è in Voi."

The conversation between Bartolomeo and Nicola regarding Salsedo's death is our interpretation of the material found in the excerpt of Green and Donahue's *Boston's Workers: A Labor History* printed in the *Boston Globe*.

For the details surrounding the arrest of Bartolomeo and Nicola, as well as the subsequent interrogations, we turned to the Avrich and Watson case histories and Musmanno's *After Twelve Years*. Ruth Johnson's recreated dialogue comes from the *Boston Herald*, "Police Obtain Clue." We also leaned heavily on Frankfurter's "Case of Sacco and Vanzetti," and Sibley's "Review of the Famous Sacco-Vanzetti Case."

The information regarding the end of the Palmer Raids is from Hochschild, "When America Tried," and the *Boston Globe*, "Anderson Orders 14 'Reds' Freed."

We built the backstory of Bartolomeo's arrest for the Bridgewater robbery from material in Sibley's "Review."

The Lewis Wade quote ("I am pretty positive . . .") is from the *Boston Globe*, "Sacco Held Without Bail."

The information about the Wall Street bombing is from the *New York Times*, "Wall Street Explosion" and "Circulars Clue to Plot."

The letter from Bartolomeo to his father is from his *Il Caso Sacco e Vanzetti* (translated by Ouisie Shapiro).

Chapter 5

The scenes inside and outside the Dedham courthouse are taken from the Watson case history and Archer's "Sacco and Vanzetti: What Really Happened?"

The backgrounds of Moore, Katzmann, and Thayer were found in the

Tejada and Watson case histories, Sibley's "Review," Grimes's "Prejudice and Politics," and Reed's "Sacco-Vanzetti Case."

The quote about Katzmann never hitting "below the belt" is from Reed's "Sacco-Vanzetti Case."

The William Thompson quote ("Your goose . . .") is from the Watson case history.

We found the information regarding the selection of a jury in the Tejada and Watson case histories, as well as Sibley's "Jury for Trial at Dedham Completed."

We re-created Judge Thayer's dialogue to summarize the goings-on in the trial. The details surrounding those exchanges can be found in the Watson case history.

The Walter Ripley quote is from William H. Daly's affidavit of September 30, 1923; we found it in Musmanno's *After Twelve Years*.

The letter from Bartolomeo to his father is from his *Il Caso Sacco e Vanzetti* (translated by Ouisie Shapiro).

Chapter 6

For most of the material in Chapter 6, we relied heavily on Sibley's coverage of the trial in the *Boston Globe* and Frankfurter's "Case of Sacco and Vanzetti."

For the testimonies of Lola Andrews, Frances Devlin, and Michael Levangie, we turned to the Massachusetts Supreme Judicial Court's online exhibit "The Case of Sacco & Vanzetti," and the trial transcripts and summaries in Fraenkel's *Sacco-Vanzetti Case*.

For the testimonies of Mary Splaine, Louis Pelser, William Proctor, and Harry Kurlansky, we referred to the transcripts found at "Sacco-Vanzetti Trial (1921)," on Linder's website, Famous Trials. For the testimony of Louis Pelser, we also leaned on the *Boston Post*, "Eye-Witnesses Fail to Identify Sacco."

The letter from Bartolomeo to his father comes from his *Il Caso Sacco e Vanzetti* (translated by Ouisie Shapiro).

Chapter 7

For the testimonies of all defense witnesses, we relied heavily on Sibley's reporting in the *Boston Globe*, as well as the trial transcripts found in Fraenkel's *Sacco-Vanzetti Case*.

Giuseppe Adrower's testimony is from Sibley's "Sacco Was in His Office."

Alfonsina Brini's testimony regarding Bartolomeo's whereabouts on April 15, 1920, is from Sibley's "Alibi for Vanzetti Offered."

The truck driver overhearing Chief Stewart say "We haven't got the right men" is from the trial transcripts; we found it in Valenti's *Question of Guilt*.

The episode in which Katzmann fires questions at the witness who said he'd been with Nicola at three o'clock on April 15 is from Sibley's "Men He Saw Not Sacco or Vanzetti."

We found Bartolomeo's testimony at "Sacco-Vanzetti Trial (1921)," on Linder's website, Famous Trials; we also relied on Sibley's "Told Untruths, Says Vanzetti."

We found Nicola's testimony at "Sacco-Vanzetti Trial (1921)," on Linder's website, Famous Trials. We also relied on Sibley's "Vanzetti Taken Ill, Trial Is Suspended."

The story about Vanzetti telling Moore to "save Nick" is from the Watson case history and Evans's *Outstanding Features*.

The quotes attributed to Judge Thayer ("get them good and proper" and "get those guys hanged") are from the *Boston Globe*, "Vanzetti Files Appeal."

Chapter 8

We summarized McAnarney's, Moore's, and Katzmann's closing arguments, all three of which can be found, verbatim, at "Sacco-Vanzetti Trial (1921)," on Linder's website, Famous Trials.

We took Judge Thayer's charge to the jury from "Sacco-Vanzetti Trial (1921)," on Linder's website, Famous Trials; we also pulled from Frankfurter's "Case of Sacco and Vanzetti" and Sibley's "Sacco and Vanzetti Both Found Guilty."

We re-created the scene in which the jury announces the verdict by pulling from a few sources, most notably "Sacco-Vanzetti Trial (1921)," on Linder's website, Famous Trials, and Sibley's "Sacco and Vanzetti Both Found Guilty."

We found Judge Thayer's quote ("Did you see what I did . . .") in Green and Donahue's "Sacco, Vanzetti, and Labor."

The letter from Bartolomeo to Elizabeth Glendower Evans is from his *Il Caso Sacco e Vanzetti* (translated by Ouisie Shapiro).

Chapter 9

The facts surrounding the Sacco-Vanzetti Defense Committee, including the worldwide response to its pleas, were gathered from the Watson case history; the *Boston Globe*, "Think Sacco and Vanzetti Persecuted"; and Spewack's reporting in the *St. Louis Post-Dispatch* and the *Pittsburgh Post*.

Felicani's quote ("I had to do something . . .") is from the Watson case history.

The newspaper quote ("Switzerland heard the cry . . .") is from Spewack's "Sacco Plea Heeded."

We found the cablegram sent by France, Barbusse, and Rolland to President Harding in the Associated Press article "French Radicals' Bomb."

Nicola's letter to comrades from November 1921 can be found in the

Aldino Felicani Sacco-Vanzetti Defense Committee Collection, online at ark.digitalcommonwealth.org/ark:/50959/tm70rg01r.

The letter from Bartolomeo to Luigia comes from his *Il Caso Sacco e Vanzetti* (translated by Ouisie Shapiro).

Chapter 10

We found the information on Moore's motions and appeals in Musmanno's *After Twelve Years* and Frankfurter's "Case of Sacco and Vanzetti." We also leaned heavily on newspapers of the day, especially the *Boston Globe*'s "'Ought to Hang' Affidavit Filed," "Police Guard Court," "Sacco-Vanzetti Arguments Over," and "Sacco and Vanzetti Denied," as well as Sibley's "Sacco-Vanzetti Case Is Postponed" and "Bill of Exceptions for Sacco Filed."

The Louis Pelser quote ("I don't think I was exactly sane . . .") is from the *Star Tribune*, "Sacco, Vanzetti Witness Says He Lied at Trial."

Lola Andrews's quotes ("unqualifiedly false . . ." and "under the intimidating . . .") are from the *Boston Globe*, "Woman Says She Gave False Testimony."

The quote from the *Boston American* ("She is either crazy . . .") was taken from the *Producers News*, "Tide Turns for Sacco and Vanzetti."

The scene in which Moore resigns is from the Watson case history and the *Boston Globe*, "Sacco-Vanzetti Counsel Quits."

The scenes showing Nicola and Bartolomeo in prison, including the birthday wishes sent by Nicola to Bartolomeo, are taken from *Letters of Sacco and Vanzetti*.

The information surrounding Madeiros's confession, including his conversation with Thompson and Judge Thayer's denying the motion, are from the Tejada and Watson case histories, Musmanno's *After Twelve Years*, and Frankfurter's "Case of Sacco and Vanzetti."

The Thayer quote about Madeiros being a crook, a thief, and a liar is from Thayer's decision in the motion for a new trial.

The Felicani quote about telegrams flooding the Defense Committee's office is taken from the excerpt of his interview at the History Matters website.

Governor Fuller's visit with Nicola, and his time with Bartolomeo, can be found in the *Boston Globe*, "Gov Fuller at State Prison." Bartolomeo's quote about Fuller talking to him like a brother can be found in the Felicani interview at the History Matters website.

The Broun quote in which he refers to Harvard as "Hangman's House" is from Shenker's "Lowell's Sacco-Vanzetti Papers."

Nicola's hunger strike is taken from the Associated Press article "Sacco Breaks Hunger Strike."

Bartolomeo's suicide attempt is taken from the Universal Service article "Vanzetti Suicide Attempt Is Foiled."

Nicola's letters to Ines and Dante are from *Letters of Sacco and Vanzetti*.

Chapter 11

For this chapter, we relied heavily on the Watson case history; the *New York Times*, "Sacco and Vanzetti Put to Death"; and the *Boston Globe*, "Madeiros, Sacco, Vanzetti Died."

Madeiros's quote ("Too bad for them . . .") is from Felicani's "Sacco-Vanzetti: A Memoir."

Nicola's conversation with Rosina ("I love you . . .") is from Musmanno's *After Twelve Years*.

The words of the United Press reporter ("The rambling old prison . . .") is from the *Dayton Herald*, "Death Stills Last Cry."

The information surrounding the protests in Europe is from the *New York Daily News,* "Café Fronts Smashed"; the *Burlington Free Press*, "Geneva Mob Hurls Imprecations"; and the *Brooklyn Daily Eagle*, "London on Guard."

We found information surrounding the funeral procession in the *Boston Globe*, "200,000 See Huge Parade."

The Elizabeth Glendower Evans quote ("They laid their bodies . . .") is from her "People I Have Known."

The *Boston Globe* quote ("As the procession proceeded . . .") is from "200,000 See Huge Parade."

The Mary Donovan quote ("One of the blackest crimes . . .") is from the Watson case history.

We found the information regarding the splitting of Nicola's and Bartolomeo's ashes in the Associated Press article "Double Burial for Sacco-Vanzetti Ashes."

The letter from Nicola and Bartolomeo to the Sacco-Vanzetti Defense Committee is from *Letters of Sacco and Vanzetti*.

Epilogue

The information regarding Luigia's grief, and the quote from her younger sister, Vincenzina ("She suffered and cried . . ."), is from the Watson case history.

The facts surrounding Rosina's life of poverty are from Shenker's "Sacco-Vanzetti Case."

Rosina's quote ("I tried it once . . .") is from the Watson case history, as is the information about Dante raising his children.

We read about the bombing of Judge Thayer's home in the Associated Press article "Bomb Menaces Life of Sacco Case Judge."

We found the information about the police guarding Katzmann's house in the Associated Press article "Sacco-Vanzetti Prosecutor."

The part about Fred Moore returning to the West can be found in the Watson case history.

Professor Frankfurter's opinion and quote were taken from his "Case of Sacco and Vanzetti."

Justice Douglas's opinion and quote, as well as Albert Einstein's quote, were taken from the Watson case history.

Governor Dukakis's proclamation, along with his quote, were taken from Shenker's "Sacco-Vanzetti Case."

BIBLIOGRAPHY

Books

Avrich, Paul. *Anarchist Voices: An Oral History of Anarchism in America*. Princeton, NJ: Princeton University Press, 1995.

———. *Sacco and Vanzetti: The Anarchist Background*. Princeton, NJ: Princeton University Press, 1991.

Christianson, Scott. *With Liberty for Some: 500 Years of Imprisonment in America*. Boston: Northeastern University Press, 1998.

Davidson, James West, and Mark Hamilton Lytle. *After the Fact: The Art of Historical Detection*. Vol. 2. New York: McGraw-Hill, 1992.

D'Attilio, Robert. "La Salute è in Voi: The Anarchist Dimension." In *Sacco-Vanzetti: Developments and Reconsiderations; 1979 Conference Proceedings*, 75–89. Boston: Trustees of the Public Library of the City of Boston, 1982.

Douglas, William O. *An Almanac of Liberty*. Garden City, NY: Doubleday, 1954.

Ehrmann, Herbert B. *The Case That Will Not Die: Commonwealth vs. Sacco and Vanzetti*. Boston: Little, Brown, 1969.

Evans, Elizabeth Glendower. *Outstanding Features of the Sacco-Vanzetti Case: Together with Letters from the Defendants*. Boston: New England Civil Liberties Committee, 1924.

Flynn, Elizabeth Gurley. *The Rebel Girl: An Autobiography; My First Life (1906–1926)*. New York: International, 1973.

Fraenkel, Osmond K. *The Sacco-Vanzetti Case*. London: Routledge, 1931. archive.org/details/in.ernet.dli.2015.221975.

Guglielmo, Jennifer, and Salvatore Salerno, eds. *Are Italians White? How Race Is Made in America*. New York: Routledge, 2003.

Guglielmo, Thomas A., "Rethinking Whiteness Historiography: The Case of Italians in Chicago, 1890–1945." In *White Out: The Continuing Significance of Racism*, edited by Ashley "Woody" Doane and Eduardo Bonilla-Silva, 48–61. New York: Routledge, 2003.

Hing, Bill Ong. *Defining America Through Immigration Policy*. Philadelphia: Temple University Press, 2004.

Joughin, Louis, and Edmund. M. Morgan. *The Legacy of Sacco and Vanzetti*. Princeton, NJ: Princeton University Press, 1948.

Kunstler, William. *Politics on Trial: Five Famous Trials of the 20th Century*. Melbourne: Ocean Press, 2003.

Murray, Robert K. *Red Scare: A Study in National Hysteria, 1919–1920*. Minneapolis: University of Minnesota Press, 1955.

Musmanno, Michael A. *After Twelve Years*. New York: Knopf, 1939.

Neville, John. *Twentieth-Century Cause Célèbre: Sacco, Vanzetti, and the Press, 1920–1927*. Westport, CT: Praeger, 2004.

Post, Louis F. *The Deportations Delirium of Nineteen-Twenty: A Personal Narrative of an Historic Official Experience*. Chicago: Kerr, 1923.

Rasenberger, Jim. *America, 1908: The Dawn of Flight, the Race to the*

Pole, the Invention of the Model T, and the Making of a Modern Nation. New York: Scribner, 2007.

Sacco, Nicola, and Bartolomeo Vanzetti. *The Letters of Sacco and Vanzetti.* Edited by Marion Denman Frankfurter and Gardner Jackson. New York: Penguin, 2007.

Sann, Paul. *The Lawless Decade: Bullets, Broads and Bathtub Gin.* Mineola, NY: Dover, 2010.

Tejada, Susan. *In Search of Sacco and Vanzetti: Double Lives, Troubled Times, and the Massachusetts Murder Case That Shook the World.* Boston: Northeastern University Press, 2012.

U.S. House of Representatives. *Hearings Relative to the Further Restriction of Immigration Before the Committee on Immigration and Naturalization,* Pt. 2, 62nd Cong., 2nd sess. Washington: Government Printing Office, 1912.

Valenti, Michael. *Question of Guilt.* New York: Paperback Library, 1966.

Vanzetti, Bartolomeo. *Il Caso Sacco e Vanzetti.* Rome: Editori Riuniti, 1962.

———. *The Story of a Proletarian Life.* Translated by Eugene Lyons. London: Kate Sharpley Library, 2001.

Wagner, Margaret E. *America and the Great War: A Library of Congress Illustrated History.* New York: Bloomsbury Press, 2017.

Watson, Bruce. *Sacco and Vanzetti: The Men, the Murders, and the Judgment of Mankind.* New York: Penguin, 2007.

Magazines and Journals

Beffel, John Nicholas. "Eels and the Electric Chair." *New Republic,* December 29, 1920.

Damon, Allan L. "The Great Red Scare." *American Heritage*, February 1968.

Evans, Elizabeth Glendower. "People I Have Known; Death and Victory." *La Follette's Magazine*, September, 1927.

Felicani, Aldino. "Sacco-Vanzetti: A Memoir." *Nation*, August 14, 1967.

France, Anatole. "Anatole France to the People of America." *Nation*, November 23, 1921.

Frankfurter, Felix. "The Case of Sacco and Vanzetti." *Atlantic*, March 1927.

Hochschild, Adam. "When America Tried to Deport Its Radicals." *New Yorker*, November 4, 2019.

Jackson, Gardner. "Sacco and Vanzetti." *Nation*, August 24, 1928.

Mostov, Stephen G. "Immigrant Entrepreneurs: Jews in the Shoe Trades in Lynn, 1885–1945." Paper prepared for the North Shore Jewish Historical Society, Marblehead, MA, 1982.

Orsi, Robert. "The Religious Boundaries of an Inbetween People: Street *Feste* and the Problem of the Dark-Skinned Other in Italian Harlem, 1920–1990." *American Quarterly* 44, no. 3 (September 1992): 313–47.

Porter, Katherine Anne. "The Never-Ending Wrong." *Atlantic*, June 1977.

Rasenberger, Jim. "1908." *Smithsonian Magazine*, January 2008.

Reed, Barry C. "The Sacco-Vanzetti Case: The Trial of the Century." *American Bar Association Journal* 46, no. 8 (August 1960): 867–72.

Russell, Francis. "The Tragedy in Dedham: A Retrospect of the Sacco-Vanzetti Trial." *Antioch Review* 15, no. 4 (Winter 1955): 387–398.

Vorse, Mary Heaton. "Sacco and Vanzetti." *World Tomorrow*, January 1921.

Zeidel, Robert F. "A 1911 Report Set America on a Path of Screening Out 'Undesirable' Immigrants." *Smithsonian Magazine*, July 16, 2018. smithsonianmag.com/history/1911-report-set-america-on-path-screening-out-undesirable-immigrants-180969636/.

Newspapers

Archer, William K. "Sacco and Vanzetti: What Really Happened?" *Courier-Journal* (Louisville, KY), August 20, 1967.

Associated Press. "Bomb Menaces Life of Sacco Case Judge." *New York Times*, September 27, 1932.

———. "Double Burial for Sacco-Vanzetti Ashes." *St. Louis Post-Dispatch*, August 30, 1927.

———. "French Radicals' Bomb Wounds 7 Policemen." *Sun* (Baltimore), October 22, 1921.

———. "Motions for Revocation of the Death Sentence and Stay of Execution Denied." *Berkshire Eagle*, August 9, 1927.

———. "Sacco Breaks Hunger Strike After 30 Days." *Chicago Tribune*, August 16, 1927.

———. "Sacco-Vanzetti Prosecutor Fatally Stricken in Court." *Fort Worth Star-Telegram*, October 16, 1953.

Baltimore Sun. "Liberal Weekly Is Outspoken Against Record of Thayer." May 20, 1927.

Berkshire Eagle. "Train Service Still Crippled as Result of Two Days' Rainstorms." July 11, 1921.

Boston Globe. "200,000 See Huge Parade." August 29, 1927.

———. "Anderson Orders 14 'Reds' Freed." June 24, 1920.

———. "Alleged Anarchist Freed, Court Questions Jurymen." April 24, 1920.

———. "Bandits Kill Guard, Shoot Paymaster, Steal $16,000." April 16, 1920.

———. "Gov Fuller at State Prison Sees Sacco and Vanzetti." July 22, 1927.

———. "Madeiros, Sacco, Vanzetti Died in Chair this Morning." August 23, 1927.

———. "'Ought to Hang' Affidavit Filed." October 2, 1923.

———. "Plain Talk to Labor and Capital." April 5, 1914.

———. "Police Guard Court at Sacco-Vanzetti Hearing." October 29, 1921.

———. "Railroad Tracks Flooded by the Torrential Rains During Electrical Storm." July 10, 1921.

———. "Real Issue Identity, Says Judge Thayer." July 14, 1921.

———. "Sacco and Vanzetti Denied New Trial." October 2, 1924.

———. "Sacco and Vanzetti Go on Trial May 31." May 29, 1921.

———. "Sacco Held Without Bail in Murder Case." May 26, 1920, Evening edition.

———. "Sacco-Vanzetti Arguments Over." November 13, 1923.

———. "Sacco-Vanzetti Counsel Quits." November 8, 1924.

———. "Sec Hoover Guest of Shoe Men Today." July 12, 1921.

———. "Think Sacco and Vanzetti Persecuted as Radicals." October 23, 1921.

———. "Vanzetti Files Appeal, Sacco Refuses to Sign." May 5, 1927.

———. "Warm Hearing on Mill Strike." March 4, 1912.

———. "Woman Says She Gave False Testimony Against Sacco." September 11, 1922.

Boston Herald. "Police Obtain Clue to More of Bandit Gang." May 8, 1920.

Boston Post. "Bandits Kill Guard and Steal $20,000." April 16, 1920.

———. "Eye-Witnesses Fail to Identify Sacco." June 11, 1921.

———. "Guilty of Murder in 1st Degree." July 15, 1921.

———. "Man Held Thought to be Bandit." April 19, 1920.

Brooklyn Eagle. "London on Guard Against New Sacco Riots as Paris and Geneva Check Damage." August 24, 1927.

Burlington Free Press. "Geneva Mob Hurls Imprecations on the United States." August 24, 1927.

———. "To Probe Leather Famine." May 12, 1916.

Daily News (New York). "Cafe Fronts Smashed by Street Mobs." August 24, 1927.

Dorsey, George A. "The Wide, Wide World." *Chicago Tribune*, August 19, 1910.

Evening Star (Washington, D.C.). "Bomb Explosion at Attorney General's Home Starts a Nation-Wide Round-Up of Anarchists." June 3, 1919.

Green, James R., and Hugh Carter Donahue. "Sacco, Vanzetti, and Labor." Excerpt of *Boston's Workers: A Labor History*. *Boston Globe*, September 1, 1997.

Grimes, William. "Prejudice and Politics: Sacco, Vanzetti, and Fear." Review of *Sacco and Vanzetti: The Men, the Murders and the Judgment of Mankind*, by Bruce Watson. *New York Times*, August 15, 2007.

Henning, Arthur Sears. "All Departments of the Government Hunt Senders of Death Missiles." *Chicago Tribune*, May 1, 1919.

Investigator. "Clew to Wall St. Bomb Wagon." *News* (New York), September 24, 1920.

———. "Wall Street Bomb Outrage Work of Boston Anarchists." *Daily News* (New York), August 25, 1921.

Kenney, John J. "How Boston Ranks Among World's Greatest Ports." *Boston Globe*, October 28, 1917.

Larson, Thomas. "The Good Shoemaker and the Poor Fish Peddler." *San Diego Reader*, August 18, 2005.

Lyons, Eugene. "Guard All Roads During New Trial of Sacco-Vanzetti." *Appeal to Reason*, November 12, 1921.

McLaughlin, Patricia. "Was Tragedy of Triangle Girls All in Vain?" *Morning Times* (Scranton, PA), March 27, 1990.

New York Times. "Bills to Punish Reds with Death." June 4, 1919.

———. "Circulars Clue to Plot." September 18, 1920.

———. "Reds Raided in Scores of Cities; 2,600 Arrests, 700 in New York; Deportation Hearings Begin Today." January 3, 1920.

———. "Sacco and Vanzetti Put to Death Early This Morning; Governor

Fuller Rejects Last-Minute Pleas for Delay After a Day of Legal Moves and Demonstrations." August 23, 1927.

———. "Wall Street Explosion Kills 30, Injures 300; Morgan Office Hit, Bomb Pieces Found; Toronto Fugitive Sent Warnings Here." September 17, 1920.

New York Tribune. "Outrages Spurred Hunt for Anarchists in U.S." January 3, 1920.

Price, Ed V. "Our Faulty Immigration System." *Chicago Tribune*, April 15, 1918.

Producers News (Plentywood, MT). "Tide Turns for Sacco and Vanzetti." September 29, 1922.

Shaub, Earl L. "Pair Spent Day of Gloom." *San Francisco Examiner*, August 23, 1927.

Shenker, Israel. "Lowell's Sacco-Vanzetti Papers Are Opened After 50 Years." *New York Times*, December 10, 1977.

———. "Sacco-Vanzetti Case Evoking Passions 50 Years After Deaths." *New York Times*, August, 23, 1977.

Sibley, Frank P. "Alibi for Vanzetti Offered at Dedham." *Boston Globe*, June 30, 1921.

———. "Bill of Exceptions for Sacco Filed." *Boston Globe*, February 11, 1922.

———. "Contradicts Evidence Given by Levangie." *Boston Globe*, July 11, 1921.

———. "Evidence Finished." *Boston Globe*, July 12, 1921.

———. "Final Pleas at Dedham Today." *Boston Globe*, July 13, 1921.

———. "Identity the Issue, Says Sacco's Counsel." *Boston Globe*, July 13 1921.

———. "Jury for Trial at Dedham Completed." *Boston Globe*, June 4, 1921.

———. "Katzmann Closes the State's Case." *Boston Globe*, July 14, 1921.

———. "Men He Saw Not Sacco or Vanzetti." *Boston Globe*, June 23, 1921.

———. "More Alibi Evidence Put In for Vanzetti." *Boston Globe*, June 30 1921.

———. "Mrs Lola Andrews Collapses." *Boston Globe*, June 13, 1921.

———. "Real Issue Identity Says Judge Thayer." *Boston Globe*, July 14, 1921.

———. "Review of the Famous Sacco-Vanzetti Case." *St. Louis Post-Dispatch*, October 28, 1921.

———. "Sacco and Vanzetti Both Found Guilty of Murder." *Boston Globe*, July 15, 1921.

———. "Sacco and Vanzetti Not in Car, He Says." *Boston Globe*, June 23, 1921.

———. "Sacco Faces Sharp Grilling on Murder." *Boston Globe*, July 8, 1921.

———. "Sacco in Boston, He Says, During Murder." *Boston Globe*, July 7, 1921.

———. "Sacco Law-Abiding Declare Employers." *Boston Globe*, July 1, 1921.

———. "Sacco Was in His Office April 15, 1920." *Boston Globe*, July 1, 1921.

———. "Sacco-Vanzetti Case Is Postponed." *Boston Globe*, March 9, 1923.

———. "Search Made of Spectators at Trial." *Boston Globe*, June 15, 1921.

———. "Thinks Sacco 'Dead Image' of Slayer." *Boston Globe*, June 10, 1921.

———. "Three Dedham Jurors Chosen." *Boston Globe*, June 1, 1921.

———. "Told Untruths, Says Vanzetti." *Boston Globe*, July 6, 1921.

———. "Vanzetti Able to Appear for Trial." *Boston Globe*, July 9, 1921.

———. "Vanzetti Further Cross-Examined." *Boston Globe*, July 6, 1921.

———. "Vanzetti Ill, Court Suspends." *Boston Globe*, July 9, 1921.

———. "Vanzetti Taken Ill, Trial Is Suspended." *Boston Globe*, July 8, 1921.

———. "Vanzetti Testifies at Murder Trial." *Boston Globe*, July 5, 1921.

———. "Witnesses Who Saw Shooting Testify." *Boston Globe*, June 24, 1921.

———. "Woman Testifies Sacco Was in Auto." *Boston Globe*, June 10, 1921.

———. "'You're a Liar,' Says Vanzetti." *Boston Globe*, June 18, 1921.

Southwick, Albert B. "Benchley Shocks Worcester!" *Worcester (MA) Telegram*, July 5, 2012.

Speer, Wm. M'Murtrie. "Nobody Held Liable for Causing Suicide." *New York Herald*, February 19, 1922.

Spewack, Samuel. "How Radicals of World Lined Up in Campaign to Save Sacco and Vanzetti." *St. Louis Post-Dispatch*, November 21, 1921.

———. "Radicals of World Respond to Cry Sent from Boston to 'Save Sacco and Vanzetti.'" *Pittsburgh Post*, November 25, 1921.

———. "Sacco Plea Heeded." *Washington Post*, November 22, 1921.

———. "'Save Sacco and Vanzetti,' Reds' Demand, Heeded." *Chicago Tribune*, November 23, 1921.

———. "Story of Propaganda to Free Sacco and Vanzetti." *St. Louis Post-Dispatch*, November 20, 1921.

St. Louis Post-Dispatch. "New Immigration Act Expected to Bring Higher Class of Aliens." June 8, 1924.

Staples, Brent. "How Italians Became 'White.'" *New York Times*, October 12, 2019.

Star Tribune (Minneapolis, MN). "Sacco, Vanzetti Witness Says He Lied at Trial." May 5, 1922.

Tobenkin, Elias. "Free Information Concerning Adopted Country the Greatest Need of Newly Arrived Immigrant." *Chicago Tribune Worker's Magazine*, March 7, 1909.

United Press. "Death Stills Last Cry of 'Long Live Anarchy' from Lips of Sacco and Friend." *Dayton Herald*, August 23, 1927.

———. "Fear More Bomb Plots." *Pittsburg Press*, September 18, 1920.

———. "Sleuths Look to Paterson and Philadelphia for Clues in Nation-Wide Bomb Plot." *Buffalo Enquirer*, June 3, 1919.

Universal Service. "Vanzetti Suicide Attempt Is Foiled." *San Francisco Examiner*, August 23, 1927.

Washington Post. "'Attempt to Terrorize Has Failed,' Palmer Says." June 4, 1919.

———. "Bomb for Hardwick." April 30, 1919.

Websites

Aldino Felicani Sacco-Vanzetti Defense Committee Collection, 1915–1977. Boston Public Library. Digital Commonwealth, Massachusetts Collections Online. digitalcommonwealth.org.

Commonwealth vs. Nicola Sacco and Bartolomeo Vanzetti. "Motion for a New Trial." October 23, 1926. digitalcommonwealth.org/book _viewer/commonwealth:hd76vk96j.

Federal Bureau of Investigation. "A Byte Out of History: The Palmer Raids." December 28, 2007. archives.fbi.gov/archives/news/stories /2007/december/palmer_122807.

Felicani, Aldino. "The Last Days Remembered: A Compatriot Recalls the Deaths of Sacco and Vanzetti in 1927." Audio excerpt of "Reminiscences of Aldino Felicani, 1954," interview by Dean Albertson, Columbia Center for Oral History. History Matters. historymatters.gmu.edu/d/108/.

Library of Congress. "Immigration and Relocation in U.S. History: Italian." Classroom Materials. loc.gov/classroom-materials /immigration/italian.

———. "Progressive Era to New Era, 1900–1929." U.S. History Primary Source Timeline. loc.gov/classroom-materials/united-states-history -primary-source-timeline/progressive-era-to-new-era-1900-1929/.

———. "Work in the Late 19th Century." Rise of Industrial America,

1876–1900. U.S. History Primary Source Timeline. loc.gov/classroom
-materials/united-states-history-primary-source-timeline/rise-of
-industrial-america-1876-1900/work-in-late-19th-century/.

Linder, Douglas O. "Sacco-Vanzetti Trial (1921)." Famous Trials.
famous-trials.com/saccovanzetti.

MacLaury, Judson. "Progressive Era Investigations." Pt. 5 of
"Government Regulation of Workers' Safety and Health, 1877–
1917." U.S. Department of Labor. dol.gov/general/aboutdol/history
/mono-regsafepart05.

Massachusetts Supreme Judicial Court. "The Case of Sacco & Vanzetti."
April 30, 2018. mass.gov/law-library/the-case-of-sacco-vanzetti.

Peters, Justin. "The Bomb-Throwing Anarchists Who Terrorized Boston
100 Years Before the Tsarnaevs." Slate, April 26, 2013. slate.com
/news-and-politics/2013/04/luigi-galleani-palmer-raids-the-bomb
-throwing-anarchists-who-terrorized-boston-100-years-before-the
-tsarnaevs.html.

Sacco Vanzetti Trial Transcripts. Digital Commonwealth: Massachusetts
Collections Online. digitalcommonwealth.org/collections/
commonwealth:j6732560x.

United States District Court for the District of Massachusetts. "Colyer v.
Skeffington." June 23, 1920. cite.case.law/f/265/17/.

IMAGE CREDITS

INDEX

Note: Page references in *italics* indicate photographs or illustrations